Windows 8 MVVM Patterns Revealed

Covers both C# and JavaScript

Ashish Ghoda

Apress·

Windows 8 MVVM Patterns Revealed

ISBN-13 (pbk): 978-1-4302-4908-5

ISBN-13 (electronic): 978-1-4302-4909-2

President and Publisher: Paul Manning
Lead Editor: Ewan Buckingham
Technical Reviewer: Fabio Claudio Ferracchiati
Editorial Board: Steve Anglin, Mark Beckner, Ewan Buckingham, Gary Cornell, Louise Corrigan, Morgan Ertel, Jonathan Gennick, Jonathan Hassell, Robert Hutchinson, Michelle Lowman, James Markham, Matthew Moodie, Jeff Olson, Jeffrey Pepper, Douglas Pundick, Ben Renow-Clarke, Dominic Shakeshaft, Gwenan Spearing, Matt Wade, Tom Welsh
Coordinating Editor: Anamika Panchoo
Copy Editor: Lori Cavanaugh
Compositor: SPi Global
Indexer: SPi Global
Artist: SPi Global
Cover Designer: Anna Ishchenko

Distributed to the book trade worldwide by Springer Science+Business Media New York, 233 Spring Street, 6th Floor, New York, NY 10013. Phone 1-800-SPRINGER, fax (201) 348-4505, e-mail orders-ny@springer-sbm.com, or visit www.springeronline.com. Apress Media, LLC is a California LLC and the sole member (owner) is Springer Science + Business Media Finance Inc (SSBM Finance Inc). SSBM Finance Inc is a **Delaware** corporation.

For information on translations, please e-mail, rights@apress.com, or visit www.apress.com.

Apress and friends of ED books may be purchased in bulk for academic, corporate, or promotional use. eBook versions and licenses are also available for most titles. For more information, reference our Special Bulk Sales–eBook Licensing web page at www.apress.com/bulk-sales.

Any source code or other supplementary materials referenced by the author in this text is available to readers at www.apress.com. For detailed information about how to locate your book's source code, go to www.apress.com/source-code/.

I dedicate this book to my grandparents (Nayansukhray and Kumud Ghoda, Mahavir and Sarala Majmudar), parents (Jitendra and Varsha Ghoda), sister (Kruti Vaishnav), and my lovely family (Pratixa, Gyan, and Anand Ghoda) whose blessings, sacrifice, continuous support, and encouragement enabled me to achieve this dream.

—Ashish Ghoda

Contents at a Glance

Contents

About the Author

Ashish Ghoda has been awarded a British Computer Society (BCS) Fellowship and is a senior IT executive with over 15 years IT leadership experience, enterprise architecture, application development, and technical and financial management.

He is a director at a Big Four auditing firm and teaches at New Jersey Institute of Technology (NJIT) and University of Maryland University College (UMUC) as adjunct assistant professor/faculty. He is also founder and president of Technology Opinion LLC providing IT services to organizations and IT community.

Ashish Ghoda is an author/co-author and technical reviewer of multiple books and articles on Microsoft platforms including *XAML Developer Reference* (Microsoft Press) and *Introducing Silverlight 4* (Apress).

He has a master's degree in information systems from NJIT and has earned Microsoft and TOGAF certifications.

About the Technical Reviewer

Fabio Claudio Ferracchiati is a senior consultant and a senior analyst/developer using Microsoft technologies. He works for Brain Force (www.brainforce.com) in its Italian branch (www.brainforce.it). He is a Microsoft Certified Solution Developer for .NET, a Microsoft Certified Application Developer for .NET, a Microsoft Certified Professional, and a prolific author and technical reviewer. Over the past ten years, he's written articles for Italian and international magazines and coauthored more than ten books on a variety of computer topics.

Acknowledgments

I would like to thank Ewan Buckingham, the lead editor of this book, who has given me opportunity to write this fast-paced guide for the new Microsoft Windows 8 application development platform.

It was a journey for me, as I learned the new concepts while writing this book and there were some unpredicted events like super storm Sandy that caused some delays. However, the support from the coordinating editor, Anamika Panchoo, and excellent feedback from the technical reviewer, Fabio Claudio Ferracchiati, and Ewan helped me to finish this book to a high standard and on time. I also would like to thank you the whole Apress team for their support during different phases of this book writing project.

Jay Nanavaty has been working with me since 2008 on different projects, including working on parts of my earlier books. This time I am happy to see him growing and becoming a significant contributor to this book. I am looking forward to seeing him becoming a co-author of my future books. I wish him good luck in his future success.

Introduction

Microsoft Windows 8 provides a new versatile platform to develop Windows 8 store applications with the "modern" touch-optimized user interface concepts running on different set of Windows 8 devices—PCs, tablets, and mobile phones.

This book provides step-by-step instructions for developing a FinanceHub Windows 8 store application using XAML and C# and HTML5, JavaScript, and CSS3 following the Model-View-View-Model (MVVM) design pattern.

This book is a fast-paced guide for how to create Windows 8 apps for PCs, tablets, and mobile phones. Whether you use C# or JavaScript, XAML, or HTML5 and CSS3, this book teaches you how to use the MVVM pattern to bring elegance, power, speed, and reusability to your Windows 8 apps. Experience in XAML and C# or HTML5, CSS3, and JavaScript would be helpful learn these concepts quickly.

Before we dive in to developing the FinanceHub Windows 8 application, let's quickly get an overview of the following:

- Model-View-View-Model (MVVM) pattern

- Windows 8 store applications

- The FinanceHub Windows 8 store application, which we are going to develop as part of this book

- The book structure

The Model-View-View-Model (MVVM) Pattern

We have established design patterns such as Model View Controller (MVC) and Model View Presenter (MVP) patterns that enable the application design to provide separation between what an application looks like (the user interface look and feel), and how the application acts on user actions (implementing the business logic and integrating with the data source). With the introduction of XAML-based frameworks and their capabilities of data binding, data templates, commands, and behaviors, an enhanced MVVM design pattern emerged, which can leverage the aforementioned XAML-based frameworks capabilities and can provide a separation between the presentation and business layers.

The MVVM pattern is mainly derived from the concept of MVC design pattern. Thus, if you are familiar with the MVC design pattern then you will see many similarities in the MVVM and MVC design patterns concepts. The MVVM pattern creates separation between these layers by allowing the user to define and implement clear role and responsibilities for the presentation and business layers and perform integration between these layers.

Figure 1 demonstrates the three main core classes—the View Class, the ViewModel Class and the Model class—of the MVVM design pattern.

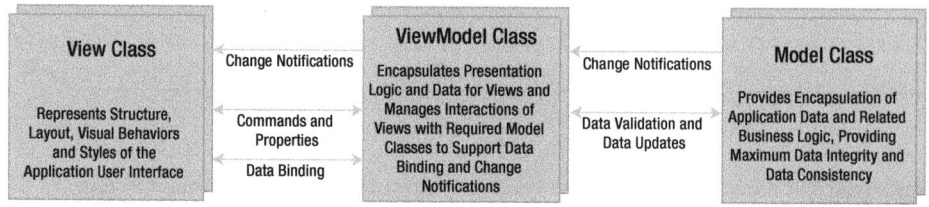

Figure 1. *Core Classes of the MVVM Design Pattern*

- View Class—defines the applications' user interface. It represents the structure, layout, visual behaviors, and styles of the application user interface. For Windows 8 store applications you can define Views of your application in XAML or HTML5. The application can contain one or more View classes as per the application requirements and application design.

- ViewModel Class—encapsulates the presentation logic and data for the view. It manages the interactions of views with the required model classes to support data binding and the change notification events by implementing required properties and commands in the ViewModel. The ViewModel class(es) do not contain any user interface. Application can contain one or more ViewModel classes as per the application requirements and application design. We will implement ViewModel classes required for the FinanceHub application, to be developed as part of this book, using C# (for the XAML-based views) and JavaScript (for HTML5-based views).

- Model Class—provides encapsulation of the application data and related business logic, allowing for maximum data integrity and data consistency. Basically it implements application data model, integrates with the data sources, and implements required business logic for data retrieval and validation in order to provide data integrity and data consistency. The Model class(es) do not contain any user interface. The application can contain one or more Model classes as per the application requirements and application design. We will implement Model classes required for the FinanceHub application, to be developed as part of this book, using C# (for the XAML-based views) and JavaScript (for HTML5-based views).

Windows 8 Store Applications

Microsoft released the latest version of the operating system Windows 8, which is designed to provide the next generation touch-optimized applications that can run seamlessly on different Windows devices from PCs and tablets, to Windows 8 mobile phones supporting different form factors. These touch-optimized, next-generation Windows 8 applications are called Windows 8 Store Applications.

The Windows 8 platform introduces a new Windows Runtime (WinRT) framework that introduces the new set of APIs and user controls for XAML and JavaScript (WinJS) to support Windows 8 store applications development. Windows 8 platform also introduces new user interface concepts, such as Charm bar and App bar, which should be considered as part of your application design.

The Windows 8 development platform enables you to develop Windows 8 store applications not only using .NET languages such as Visual Basic .NET and C# and XAML to define the presentation layer but also using more generic languages such as C++ and JavaScript and HTML5 and CSS3 to define the presentation layer. You must install Windows 8 and Visual Studio 2012 to develop Windows 8 applications.

Please note that in this book I will be using "Windows 8 store application" and "Windows 8 application" words interchangeably.

The FinanceHub Windows 8 Store Application

We are going to develop a FinanceHub Windows 8 store application using XAML and C# and HTML5, CSS3 and JavaScript using Visual Studio Windows store default XAML and JavaScript application project templates to demonstrate how to best implement MVVM design pattern for Windows 8 apps.

The FinanceHub application allows you to add/remove stocks to create a stocks watchlist to monitor your favorite stocks. The application contains two main views:

- The first view is a home page, showing your favorite stocks with the latest updates in the stock price.

- The second view is a stock details view, which provides the detailed information of the selected stock.

It will also implement a Windows 8 appbar to allow add and remove one or more stocks from your watchlist.

Figure 2 shows the home page and Figure 3 shows the stocks details page of the FinanceHub Windows 8 application.

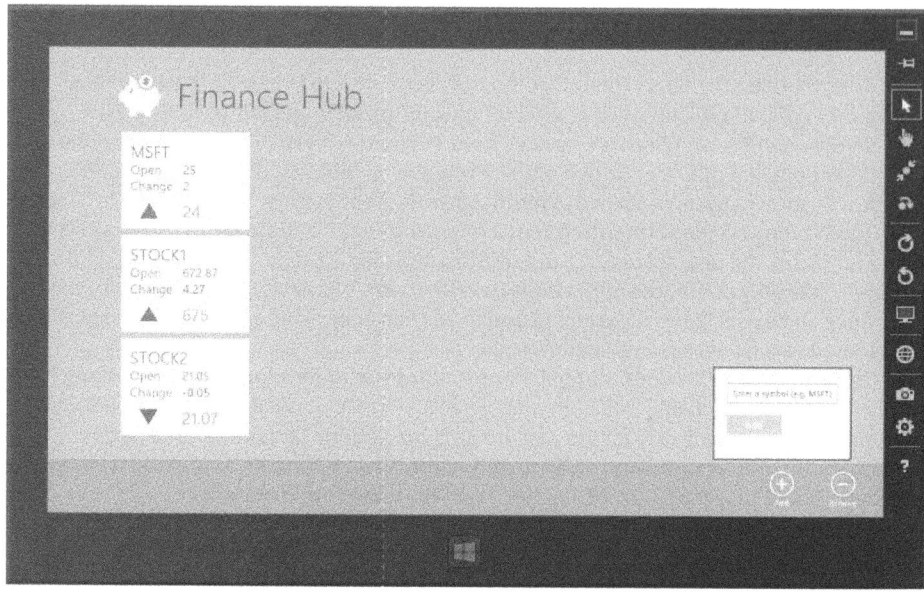

Figure 2. *Home Page of the FinanceHub Windows 8 store application displaying the stocks watchlist and an appbar with Add Stock flyout*

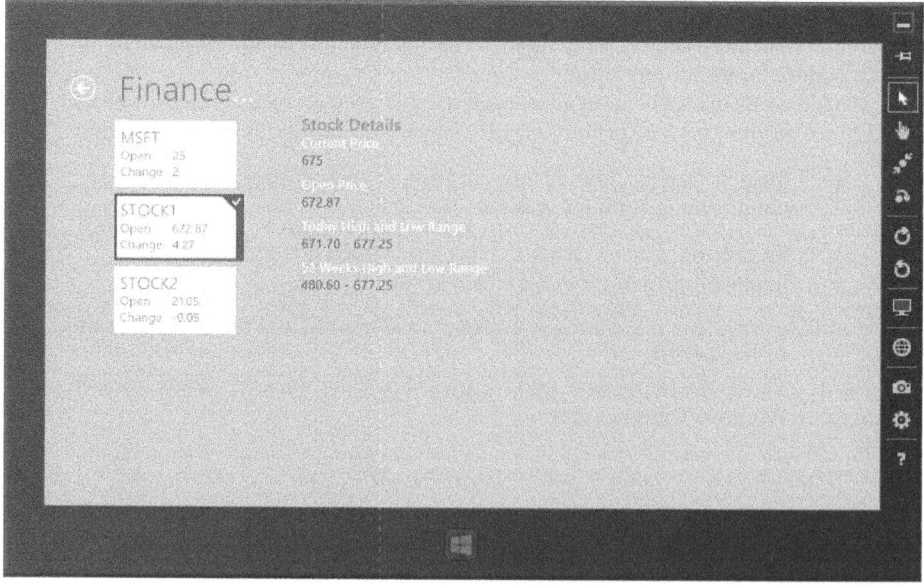

Figure 3. *Stock Details Page of the FinanceHub Windows 8 store application displaying selected stock information*

The Book Structure

This book contains six chapters.

- The first four chapters are focused on developing the FinanceHub Windows 8 application using XAML and C# following MVVM design pattern.

- Chapters 5 and 6 will describe how to develop the FinanceHub Windows 8 application using HTML5, CSS3, and JavaScript following MVVM design pattern.

Chapter 1: Setting Up Windows 8 Application Project

The first chapter provides information on how to set up your development environment to start the Windows 8 application development. It will also create a skeleton of the FinanceHub XAML Windows 8 application that would require the user to follow and implement the MVVM design pattern.

Chapter 2: Implementing the View

The second chapter will implement required view classes to build the user interface (home page, stock details view, appbar, and add and remove stocks view) of the FinanceHub application following the hierarchical navigation pattern. Along with building the user interface, we will explore some of the key enhancements made in the XAML and some of the new properties introduced in WinRT.

Chapter 3: Implementing the Model

The third chapter will implement lightweight model classes that defined the serializable and deserializable stocks data model and will also implement pre-requisites to implement features of Add and Remove stock actions. During the implementation we will explore and use some of the new features introduced in the .NET Framework 4.5.

Chapter 4: Implementing the ViewModel

The fourth chapter will implement the ViewModel classes to support stocks information binding to StocksPage, StockDetails, and RemoveStock views, and application navigation. It will also implement action commands to support stock selection and add and remove stock actions. We will also revisit the earlier implementation of the project to remove the hard-coded information and bind it to the ViewModel properties and commands.

Chapter 5: HTML5, JavaScript, and Windows 8 Applications

The fifth chapter will provide a quick overview of HTML5, JavaScript, and best practices to develop JavaScript program. We will also look at Microsoft Windows 8 development platform and development tools to support development of Windows 8 store applications using HTML5 and JavaScript.

Chapter 6: View, Model, and ViewModel Structures in HTML5 and JavaScript

The sixth and final chapter of the book will create a navigation template-based Windows 8 JavaScript application project and set up the structure to support MVVM-based implementation. We will implement the View, Model, and ViewModel of the FinanceHub application with all features that were also implemented using XAML and C# in the earlier chapters of this book.

The Source Code

You can download complete source code of this book from the Apress website. The source code contains code for each chapter within the related chapter number folder. Some chapters may contain subfolders to demonstrate step-by-step implementation.

CHAPTER 1

▓ ▓ ▓

Setting Up Windows 8 Application Project

Aren't you excited to get your first hands-on experience by developing FinanceHub Windows 8 application following MVVM design pattern? This chapter will guide you through setting up the development environment and then we will create a FinanceHub Windows 8 application project using one of the Visual Studio Windows Store XAML templates and will set up project structure supporting MVVM pattern-based development. Let's get started!

The Development Environment

Microsoft has tried very hard to make the development experience smoother with the next generation of its integrated development tool sets. You need to follow four simple steps to set up your Visual Studio 2012 development environment for developing Windows 8 applications.

1. Install Windows 8 Operating System.

2. Install Visual Studio 2012 (recommended for this book) or Visual Studio 2012 Express for Windows 8.

3. Set up required Database Storage platform.

4. Obtain Developer License

The Windows 8 Operating System

The first step is to install Windows 8. This is a mandatory step and for the Windows 8 application development you must install Windows 8 operating system. If you have not done so please visit the Microsoft Windows 8 home page (http://windows.microsoft.com/en-US/windows/home) and set up your machine with Windows 8.

Windows 8 applications will only run on the Windows 8 platform; thus it's important to note that so far Microsoft has not allowed the development of the Windows 8 applications for earlier Windows operating system such as Windows 7 and Windows Vista as well as server-side operating systems such as Windows 2012 server and Windows 2008 server.

The Visual Studio Development Platform

Windows 8 applications development is supported only on the latest version of Visual Studio (Visual Studio 2012). You have the option to either install a full version of Visual Studio 2012 or the Express edition of the Visual Studio 2012 for Windows 8. Let's look at both options in turn.

> ■ **Note**   For this book I have used Visual Studio 2012 Ultimate edition. However, you can use any of the below mentioned Visual Studio 2012 versions to develop the project in this book.

Visual Studio 2012

You can use Visual Studio 2012 Ultimate, Premium, or Professional version to build a line of business enterprise applications. Install Visual Studio 2012 (one of the mentioned versions – based on the license available to you), which will also install the following required components to develop Windows 8 applications:

- Windows 8 SDK

- Blend for Visual Studio

- Windows 8 XAML and JavaScript Project Templates

The Visual Studio Ultimate 2012 version comes with the all possible features in all areas. Compared to the Ultimate version the Premium version lacks some of the features in the areas of debugging and diagnostic, testing tools, and architecture and modeling. Whereas the Professional version lacks more features in the areas of debugging and diagnostic, integrated environment, testing, tools, architecture and modeling, Team Foundation Server, software and services for production use, and software for development and testing.

> ■ **Note**   Get details on feature comparisons in the above-mentioned areas between different versions of Visual Studio 2012 by visiting Microsoft site -
> http://www.microsoft.com/visualstudio/11/en-us/products/compare.

Visual Studio 2012 Express for Windows 8

You can also use Visual Studio 2012 Express for Windows 8 to build a professional Windows 8 application. The Express Visual Studio edition is free to developers. Install Visual Studio 2012 Express for Windows 8 from the Microsoft website (http://www.microsoft.com/visualstudio/11/en-us/products/express), which will also install the following required components to develop Windows 8 applications:

- Windows 8 SDK

- Blend for Visual Studio

- Windows Store XAML and JavaScript Project Templates

Data Storage

The FinanceHub Windows 8 application will need to store stock portfolio and other related information. We will use a CSV (comma separated values) file to store the required information for demonstration purposes in this book. However, for other line of business (LoB) applications you can determine whether using SQL Server or a similar type of scalable database platform for the information storage would be more suitable.

Note   Refer to "Pro Windows 8 Development with XAML and C#" by Jesse Liberty to get more information of how you develop LoB Windows 8 applications with database integration. Visit http://www.apress.com/microsoft/visual-studio/9781430240471 to get more information on this book.

Developer License

You must obtain a developer license to develop, build, install, and test Windows 8 applications before submitting them to the Windows Store for testing and certification. The developer license is free and you can obtain one or more developer licenses. There are two ways you can receive a developer license:

- Using Visual Studio 2012, where you will be asked to obtain a developer license when you install Visual Studio 2012 on your machine and then open it for the first time.

- Using Windows PowerShell commands from the command prompt, which you will use typically when you have not installed Visual Studio 2012.

Note   Visit the Microsoft MSDN site at http://msdn.microsoft.com/en-us/library/windows/apps/hh974578 to get more details on the developer license, especially if you have to get it via command prompt, which is not the case in this book.

The Windows Store Project Templates

Visual Studio 2012 provides a few default Windows Store project templates that will give you a head start developing your applications. You'll find templates for both XAML and .NET languages as well HTML5 and JavaScript. Some of the common Windows 8 store application project templates across different languages are:

- Blank App – project template is a single-page project, which does not contain any predefined controls or layout, namely, user interface.

- Grid App – project template is a multi-page project that allows navigation among group items and group-level dedicated page displays group and related items. You would use this template when you look at set of categories (group) of the application content and then drill through in details by displaying selected category (group) and related lists of items and so on. Windows 8 App Store and Video applications are examples of Grid template-based applications.

- Split App – project template is a two-page project where the first page displays groups and enables you to select one of the groups, which will display the second page containing a list of items and the details of the selected item on the right side. You would use this template when you want to quickly look at the list of items and details of the selected item on the right side in a two-column view. Windows news reader and email applications are examples of Split template-based applications. In this book I will be using Blank App project template to develop the FinanceHub application to demonstrate everything from scratch.

Creating a Windows Store XAML Project – FinanceHub

This section will create a Windows 8 XAML project - FinanceHub - using the Windows Store Blank App project template. Next we will explore and understand the project structure, default files, and the package application manifest file. Finally we will create new folders supporting the development of the application using MVVM design-pattern. At the end of the chapter you'll be left with a strong foundation on which you'll build through the remainder of this tutorial.

1. As shown in Figure 1-1, to create a new project named FinanceHub select Visual C# and the Windows Store option under the Installed Templates section of the Visual Studio New Project window.

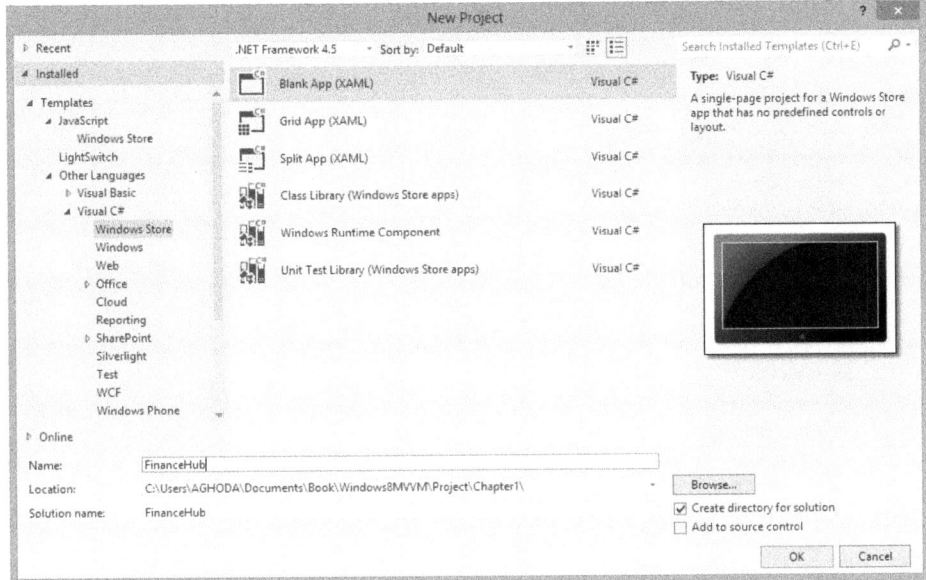

Figure 1-1. *Creating Windows Store XAML Project in Visual Studio 2012 using the Blank App Project Template*

2. You will see a set of XAML project templates from which you should select Blank App (XAML) option.

3. Set the Name of the project to FinanceHub and select an appropriate location and click OK to create the project.

You will see that a new folder FinanceHub is created and the project is created under that folder.

Exploring FinanceHub Project

If you open the FinanceHub project and look at the Solution Explorer window you will find a familiar WPF and Silverlight-like project structure, as shown in Figure 1-2.

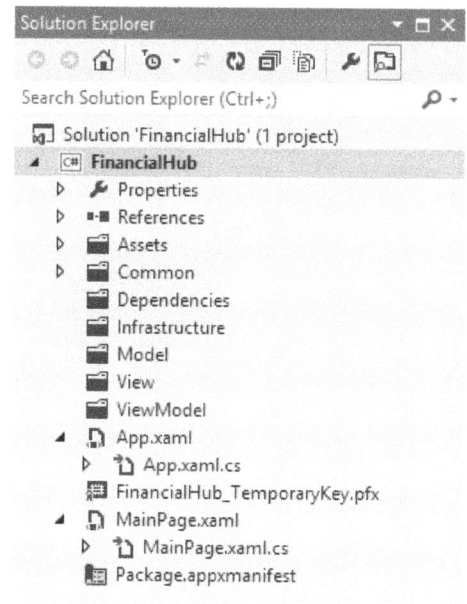

Figure 1-2. *Default FinanceHub Project Structure*

The Project Structure

You will see some familiar XAML project structure as well a few new things introduced for Windows 8 applications. Let's quickly look at each of them:

- App.xaml and MainPage.xaml and related code-behind files are similar to any other WPF and Silverlight XAML projects.

- Under Common folder there is a single helper file StandardStyle.xaml, which contains the set of styles that are common for Windows 8 application layout.

- Under Assets folder a set of 4 PNG icon images are present that are used by the application manifest defining default application logos (large and small application logos to display on the start screen and application logo to be displayed on the Windows Store) and splash screen (to display when the application starts).

- Visual Studio 2012 enables adding reference to the whole SDK rather individual assemblies. As a result you will see by default References folder contains two SDK files, which actually references all the assemblies as part of the attached SDK. First SDK reference is to the .NET for Windows 8 apps that essentially references all new Windows 8 APIs. Second SDK reference is to the Windows SDK that references to all .NET Windows System Assembly files.

6

- Under `Properties` folder you will see an `AssemblyInfo.cs` file, which includes general information about the application.

The Package Application Manifest File

The `Package.appxmanifest` file is an important file, which defines the runtime configuration properties and enables the capabilities of the Windows 8 application deployment package. When you open this file within Visual Studio 2012, it will open as a window with four tabs: Application UI, Capabilities, Declarations, and Packaging.

The Application UI Tab

Figure 1-3 shows the Application UI tab that will allow you to set the properties that describe your application. The application properties include the application entry point, startup icon, preferred application orientation, and application splash screen definition. It references images stored under the `Assets` folder of the project.

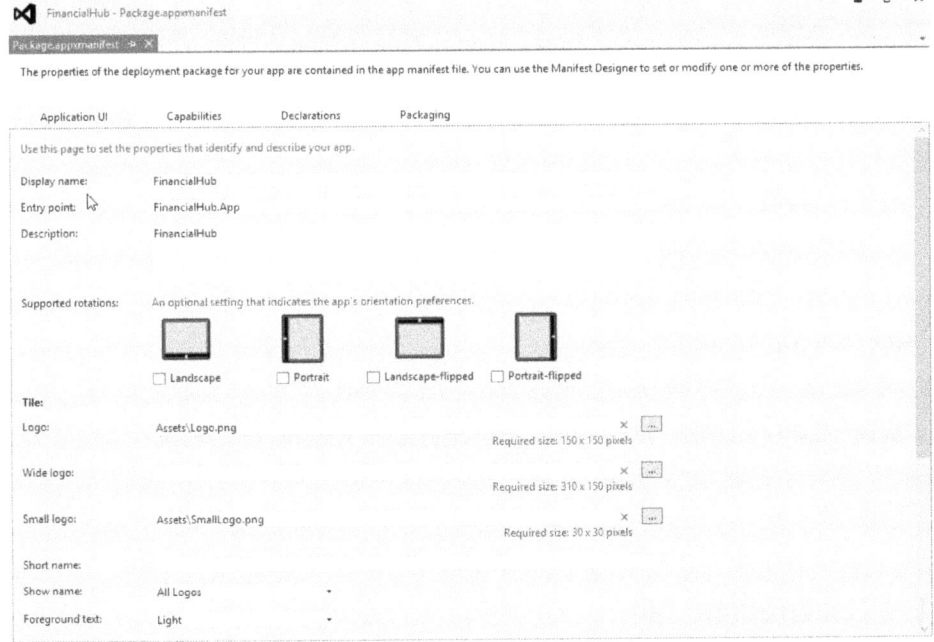

Figure 1-3. *The Application UI Tab*

The Capabilities Tab

Figure 1-4 shows the Capabilities tab, which is introduced for Windows 8 applications. This tab will enable application features such as access to Document Libraries, Internet, Microphone, Location, and Webcam. You must check the associated checkbox to enable this feature during application execution.

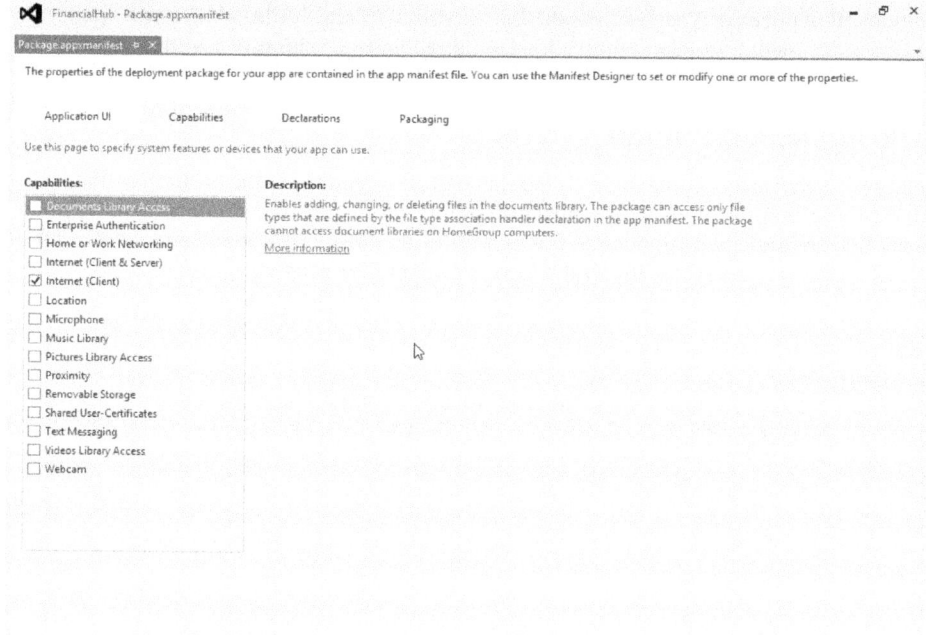

Figure 1-4. *The Capabilities Tab*

■ **Note** Even if you have written code associated to the feature and have not selected the related feature under the Capabilities tab, the feature will not be available to the deployed application.

The Declarations Tab

Figure 1-5 shows the Declarations tab, which is introduced for Windows 8 applications. This tab will enable you to add declarations and specify related properties enabling integration of your application with other applications such as the Search contract. The Search contract will allow you to add a Search pane to your application and you can search within and across application content. It will also allow other applications to search your application content.

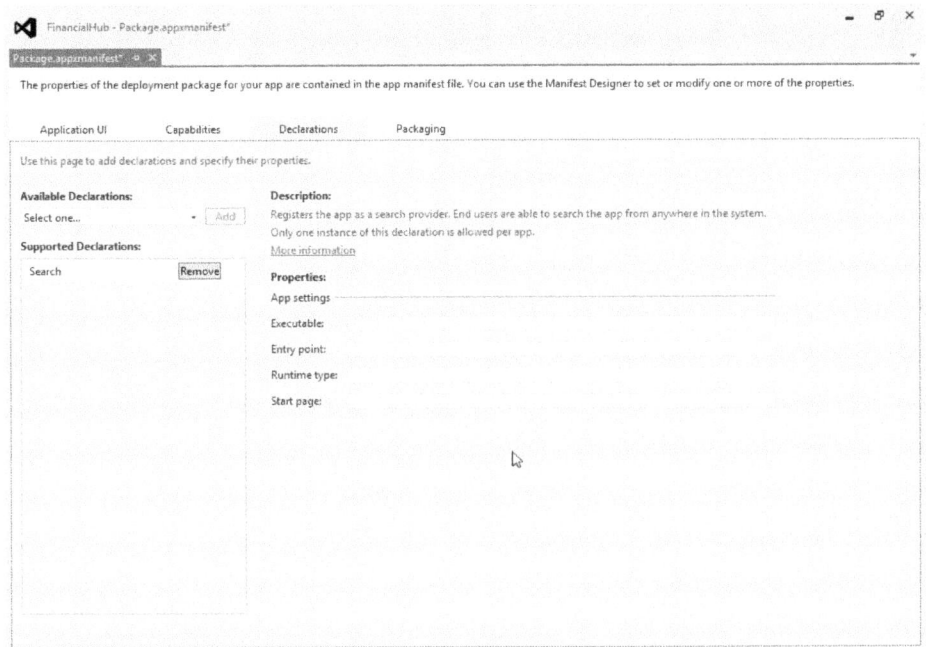

Figure 1-5. *The Declaration Tab*

The Packaging Tab

Figure 1-6 shows the Packaging tab, which describes the application deployment package, allowing you to update key package properties such as package identification id, windows store logo (the image is added under the Assets folder), application version, and publisher information.

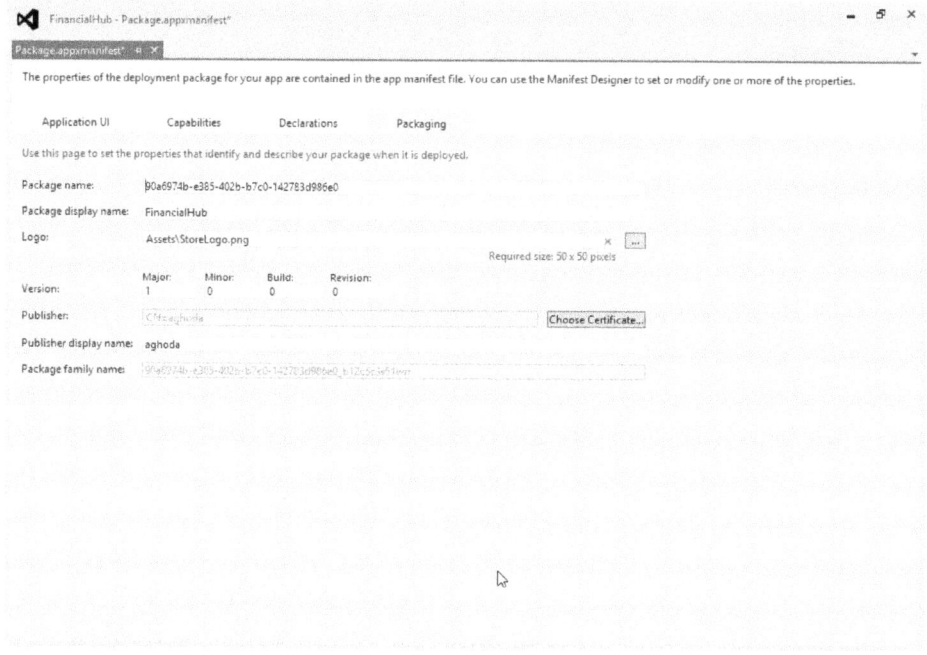

Figure 1-6. The Packaging Tab

Setting MVVM Architecture in FinanceHub Project

So far we looked at the default blank XAML Windows Store application structure. Next we will add some additional folders to support the design and development of the FinanceHub project using MVVM design pattern.

Please add the following five folders as placeholders to support the MVVM design pattern:

- Dependencies – This folder will contain additional third party or custom dependencies assemblies that would require development of our application.

- Infrastructure – This folder will contain required classes and will implement services to support loosely coupled MVVM development.

- Model – This folder will contain the model class of the application.

- View – This folder will contain the user interface definition made up of different XAML controls and pages of the application.

- ViewModel – This folder will contain the ViewModel of the pages/usercontrols.

Figure 1-7 shows the final blank project structure of the FinanceHub Windows 8 application.

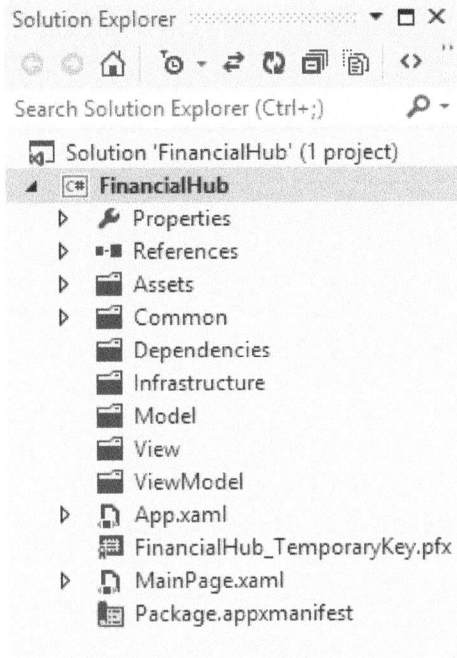

Figure 1-7. *Final FinanceHub Application Project Structure*

If you run the project at this point, it will compile successfully and you will see the project is running without any user interface.

Summary

You have now seen how to set up your development environment to start the Windows 8 application development. As you noticed Windows 8 and Visual Studio 2012 are required to develop Windows 8 applications. You even have an option to use Visual Studio 2012 Express, though I recommend using one of the regular Visual Studio 2012 versions to develop LoB Windows 8 applications.

The first chapter of this book ended with creating a skeleton of the FinanceHub XAML Windows 8 application that will follow and implement the MVVM design pattern in the next three chapters. We used the Windows Store Blank XAML App project template in Visual Studio 2012. We also added a few blank folders as placeholders to support the development following the MVVM design pattern.

Do not forget to download the source code and visit the Chapter1 folder to view the source code that we developed in this chapter.

The next chapter defines the presentation layer, or the view of the application that will drive the user interface of the application.

CHAPTER 2

Implementing the View

The main objective of following the MVVM design pattern is to provide separation between what an application looks like (the user interface look and feel), and how the application acts on user actions (implementing the business logic and integrating with the data source). After creating a blank XAML Windows 8 application in Chapter 1, we need to define the presentation layer of the FinanceHub application. The View represents the definition of the applications' user interface in MVVM design pattern. This chapter will focus on how the application looks, so we will be mainly focusing on the following points with minimal focus on the code-behind:

- Defining application deployment package and runtime configuration properties

- Defining the resources to drive styles and themes of the application

- Developing application user interface (the view) using XAML

You will be updating the blank project further to define the view of the FinanceHub application.

Customizing Deployment Package and Runtime Configuration Properties

It's odd to set up the deployment package and runtime configuration properties in the beginning but it's a good practice to decide your application deployment properties up front to match your application's features and functionalities as well as the application color scheme theme. This is getting more important since you are deploying applications to app stores (in our case, Windows Application Store) and you want to make sure that your application deployment design is considered from the beginning. With this approach you can create a compelling end-to-end branding story making your application more visible and attractive. The other point you need to consider from the beginning is the minimum requirements and qualifications your application needs to meet in order to publish your application to specific app stores. These can vary by app store (e.g., Windows app store vs. Apple's and Google's). At present for Windows app store the minimum requirement is to provide custom application–specific app logos and color scheme; otherwise you will see the default ones. Let's start!

In Windows 8 application, the `Package.appxmanifest` file manages deployment application package and runtime configuration properties. For the FinanceHub application project we will change the background color of the tile and different application logos. Open the blank project you created as part of Chapter 1 to get started.

Background Color of the Tile

I am going to select a light tile background color instead of the default dark tile background color for this project. In order to keep the overall color scheme in sync, we need to change the background color for the splash screen. To customize the splash screen background color; open `Package.appxmanifest` file and you will see four tabs. The first default tab is Application UI tab; in which you should notice Hex color value #464646 for Background Color under the Tile section. This Hex code represents dark gray color. Change it to the value #9ea7b1, which represents a light gray shade.

Application Logo Files and Splash Screen

The next step is to provide its own branding to the FinanceHub application by defining different application logos and the splash screen. For that you will be replacing default logo image files with the custom ones.

If you visit the `Assets` folder displayed in the Solution Explorer window; you will notice that there four logo image files were added as part of the default project:

- `Logo.png` – is 150x150 pixel PNG type image file represents the main Tile logo and is referenced as Tile logo under the Application UI tab of the `Package.appxmanifest` file

- `SmallLogo.png` – is 30x30 pixel PNG type image file represents the small tile logo and is referenced as Tile Small logo under the Application UI tab of the `Package.appxmanifest` file

- `SplashScreen.png` – is 620x300 pixel PNG type image file represents a splash screen of the application and is referenced as Splash Screen under the Application UI tab of the `Package.appxmanifest` file

- `StoreLogo.png` – is 50x50 pixel PNG type image file represents the deployed application logo, which displayed in Windows Store, and is referenced as Logo under the Packaging tab of the `Package.appxmanifest` file

I have chosen the piggy bank concept to brand the FinanceHub project and thus need to create appropriate PNG file type images with the required sizes that will replace the above-mentioned image files under the `Assets` folder. You can delete the existing logo and splash screen files and add your custom ones (with the same file name, file type, and file size) using Add ➤ Existing Item option within the solution explorer window. Now you are ready to provide your own brand to the application.

■ **Note** You must keep custom logo and custom splash screen images as PNG file types with the above-mentioned names and image file sizes. Changes in that area will be reported as an error.

Visit Package.appxmanifest file's Application UI and Packaging tab. If you have added the right logo files and splash screen you should not see any red X signs; otherwise you will see a red X sign explaining the problem. For demonstration purposes, I have replaced StoreLogo.png file with 80x80 file size rather than the 50x50 required file size. Now if you visit the Packaging tab, you will notice an error, as shown in Figure 2-1.

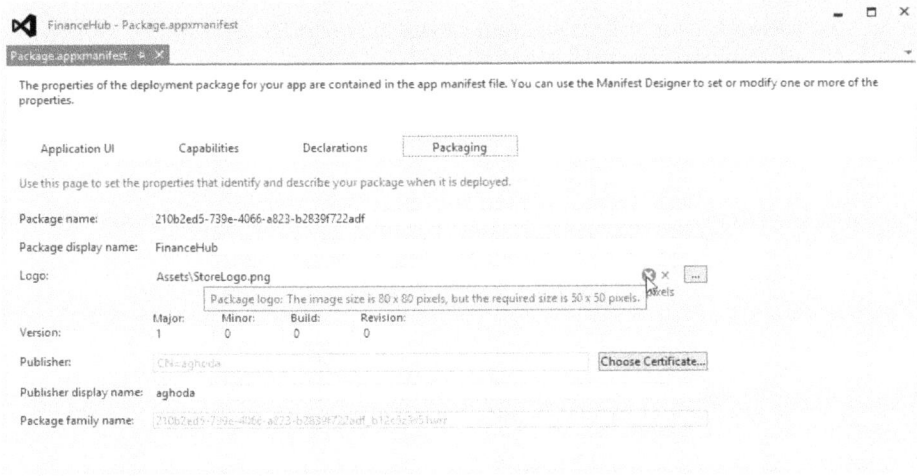

Figure 2-1. *Demonstrating Error when the added StoreLogo.png file does not contain the required 50x50 size*

At this point if you run the application; you should see a custom splash screen with our newly defined custom light background and the application without any tiles (just a blank screen) with the default dark color theme.

Enabling Customization of Application Styles and Themes

Consistent styling and theming across your application helps in providing a consistent user experience to your application users. Externalizing definition of application styles and themes as resources simplify the management and maintenance of application styling and theming.

You might have noticed that under Common folder there is a single helper file StandardStyle.xaml, which contains the set of styles that are common for Windows 8 application layout. If you open that file you will notice that Microsoft recommends not to alter this particular file and instead create a separate similar resource dictionary file that contains variations to these default styles by overriding them. You can also introduce new sets of styles based on the requirements of your application.

Adding New Resource Dictionary File

To add a new resource dictionary file, which will be used to override the default application styles and add new additional styles:

1. Select the Common folder in the Solution Explorer windows and right click to add new item.

2. Select Resource Dictionary item and name the file to Resources.xaml as shown in Figure 2-2.

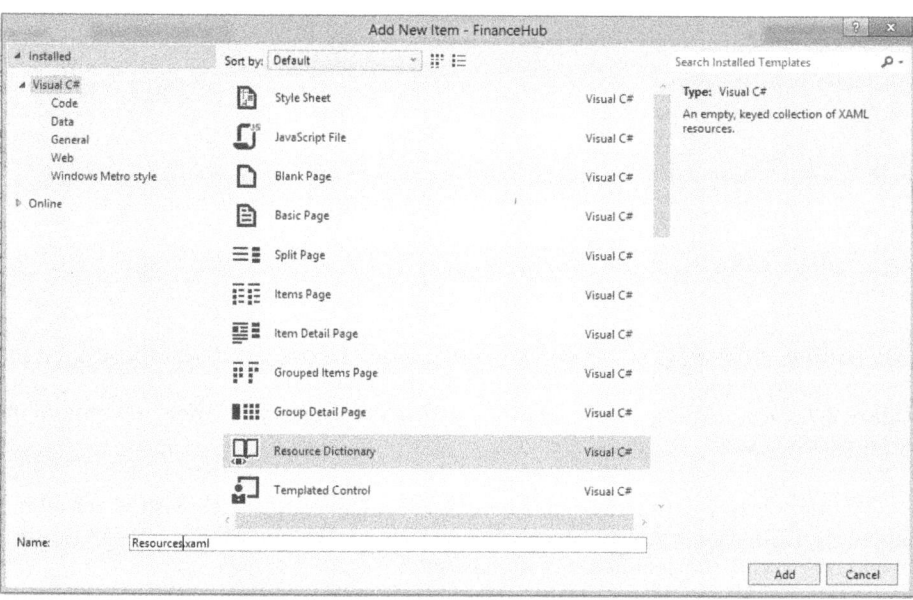

Figure 2-2. *Adding New Resouces.xaml Resource Dictionary File*

The newly added Resources.xaml resource dictionary file is a blank file with default namespace declaration as shown below.

```
<ResourceDictionary
    xmlns="http://schemas.microsoft.com/winfx/2006/xaml/presentation"
    xmlns:x="http://schemas.microsoft.com/winfx/2006/xaml"
    xmlns:local="using:FinanceHub.Common">

</ResourceDictionary>
```

■ **Enhancements in XAML**   You will notice the using key word in defining the namespace in the above code snippet. With Windows 8, the XAML platform is enhanced and is available to the native environment making XAML platform a language agnostic platform (e.g., available to C++ also). As a result, XAML namespace declaration approach is changed to be more language agnostic and instead of using clr-namespace now you will be using the using keyword to decorate the namespace within XAML.

Enabling Additional Resources.xaml Resource Dictionary at Application Level

The next step is to create the Resources.xaml resource dictionary visible at the application level. For that you add ResourceDictionary, with the Source value set to the newly added Resources.xaml file, to the generic collection referenced by MergedDictionaries within the App.xaml file, as shown below.

```
<Application.Resources>
    <ResourceDictionary>
        <ResourceDictionary.MergedDictionaries>
            <!--
                Styles that define common aspects of the platform
                    look and feel
                Required by Visual Studio project and item
                    templates
            -->
            <ResourceDictionary
                Source="Common/StandardStyles.xaml"/>
            <ResourceDictionary Source="Common/Resources.xaml"/>
        </ResourceDictionary.MergedDictionaries>
    </ResourceDictionary>
</Application.Resources>
```

■ **Note**   Please note the order of the added ResourceDictionary element for Resources.xaml file. It is added immediately after the StandardStyles.xaml file as a last ResourceDictionary to the MergedDictionaries collection. During execution the last added ResourceDictionary to the MergedDictionaries collection will be searched first and thus if you are overriding style values with the same key name; that resource file should be added last to the collection (we'll get to key names in the next section).

Customizing Application Theme

Windows 8 SDK provides three pre-defined Windows 8 application themes – light, dark, and high contrast – that are defined in the themeresources.xaml file that will be applicable to Windows 8 applications developed using XAML.

The default Windows 8 application theme is a dark color theme and for that you do not need to set anything. However, you can select dark and light color themes by assigning `Application.RequestedTheme` property to `Dark` or `Light` value within `App.xaml` file, as shown below:

Programmatically Setting Light Color Theme

```
<Application
    x:Class="FinanceHub.App"
    xmlns=
        "http://schemas.microsoft.com/winfx/2006/xaml/presentation"
    xmlns:x="http://schemas.microsoft.com/winfx/2006/xaml"
    xmlns:local="using:FinanceHub"
    RequestedTheme="Light">
```

Programmatically Setting Dark Color Theme

```
<Application
    x:Class="FinanceHub.App"
    xmlns=
        "http://schemas.microsoft.com/winfx/2006/xaml/presentation"
    xmlns:x="http://schemas.microsoft.com/winfx/2006/xaml"
    xmlns:local="using:FinanceHub"
    RequestedTheme="Dark">
```

The High Contrast theme is automatically activated by Windows once the corresponding option is selected in the Control Panel.

■ **Note**   You can locate `themeresources.xaml` file at `C:\Program Files (x86)\Windows Kits\8.0\Include\winrt\xaml\design` for 64-bit OS and `C:\Program Files\Windows Kits\8.0\Include\winrt\xaml\design` for 32-bit OS. I highly recommend you quickly go through these styles to get idea of different types of controls and related style definitions in the Windows 8 application.

We will change the default dark color theme to a custom light color theme. For FinanceHub application we would need to override theme resources related to AppBar, ApplicationPage Background and ProgressBar, ComboBox, and ListView controls by adding light color values with the Key name values in the newly added `Resources.xaml` file, which are same as the key name values defined in the `themeresources.xaml` file. The following code snippet demonstrates this configuration:

```
<!--Color resources-->
<Color x:Key="AppPurpleColor">#FF585A8E</Color>
<Color x:Key="AppLightPurpleColor">#6a7bba</Color>
```

```xml
<!--Theme overrides-->
<SolidColorBrush
    x:Key="AppBarBackgroundThemeBrush"
    Color="#9ea7b1" />
<SolidColorBrush
    x:Key="AppBarBorderThemeBrush"
    Color="#93a8c8" />
<SolidColorBrush
    x:Key="ApplicationPageBackgroundThemeBrush"
    Color="#B3BDE1"/>
<SolidColorBrush
    x:Key="ProgressBarIndeterminateForegroundThemeBrush"
    Color="{StaticResource AppPurpleColor}" />
<SolidColorBrush
    x:Key="ComboBoxItemSelectedBackgroundThemeBrush"
    Color="{StaticResource AppPurpleColor}" />
<SolidColorBrush
    x:Key="ComboBoxItemSelectedForegroundThemeBrush"
    Color="White" />
<SolidColorBrush
    x:Key="ComboBoxItemSelectedPointerOverBackgroundThemeBrush"
    Color="{StaticResource AppPurpleColor}" />
<SolidColorBrush
    x:Key="ComboBoxSelectedBackgroundThemeBrush"
    Color="{StaticResource AppPurpleColor}" />
<SolidColorBrush
    x:Key="ComboBoxSelectedPointerOverBackgroundThemeBrush"
    Color="{StaticResource AppPurpleColor}" />
<SolidColorBrush
    x:Key="ListViewItemPlaceholderBackgroundThemeBrush"
    Color="{StaticResource AppPurpleColor}" />
<SolidColorBrush
    x:Key="ListViewItemSelectedBackgroundThemeBrush"
    Color="{StaticResource AppPurpleColor}" />
<SolidColorBrush
    x:Key="ListViewItemSelectedPointerOverBackgroundThemeBrush"
    Color="{StaticResource AppPurpleColor}" />
<SolidColorBrush
    x:Key="ListViewItemSelectedPointerOverBorderThemeBrush"
    Color="{StaticResource AppPurpleColor}" />
```

Next you need to open the StandardStyles.xaml resource file, which is available under the Common folder and merge Resources.xaml dictionary with the default theme dictionary by adding the following markup.

```xml
<ResourceDictionary.ThemeDictionaries>
    <ResourceDictionary x:Key="Default">
        <x:String x:Key="BackButtonGlyph">&#xE071;</x:String>
```

```
<x:String
    x:Key="BackButtonSnappedGlyph">&#xE0BA;</x:String>
<ResourceDictionary.MergedDictionaries>
    <ResourceDictionary Source="Resources.xaml"/>
</ResourceDictionary.MergedDictionaries>
</ResourceDictionary>
....
```

Now if you run the project you will notice that the application page background has changed to the light gray color, which was set as custom theme color, instead of the dark gray color.

This exercise is also a great start to make a place holder for future customization of styles related to the application. We will update the Resources.xaml file as we continue developing the view of the application throughout the remaining chapter.

Developing User Interface

Let's build a user interface for the FinanceHub application by adding the required XAML pages as views under the View folder.

The Main Startup Page – MainPage.xaml

We will be treating MainPage.xaml as the main page container that you can compare as a master page for any ASP.NET application or shell of the Prism framework. For that under the View folder Add Blank Page item with the name set to MainPage.xaml as shown in Figure 2-3.

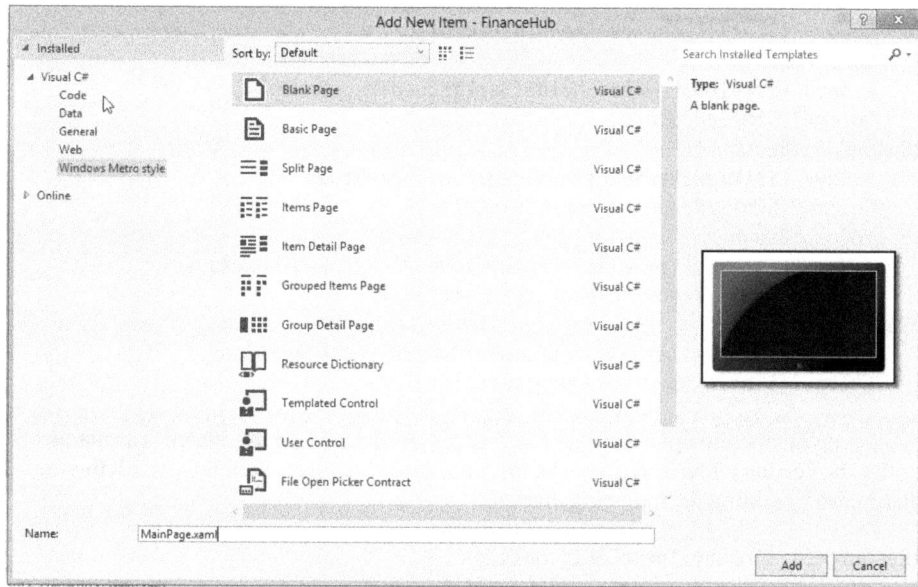

Figure 2-3. *Adding New XAML Blank Page as MainPage.xaml under View folder*

This page definition, as shown below, is very much similar to the original MainPage.xaml file, which still exists in the root folder.

```
<Page
    x:Class="FinanceHub.View.MainPage"
    IsTabStop="false"
    xmlns="http://schemas.microsoft.com/winfx/2006/xaml/presentation"
    xmlns:x="http://schemas.microsoft.com/winfx/2006/xaml"
    xmlns:local="using:FinanceHub.View"
    xmlns:d="http://schemas.microsoft.com/expression/blend/2008"
    xmlns:mc=
      "http://schemas.openxmlformats.org/markup-compatibility/2006"
    mc:Ignorable="d" Margin="-1,0,1,0">

    <Grid Background="{StaticResource
          ApplicationPageBackgroundThemeBrush}">

    </Grid>
</Page>
```

You do not need to keep two MainPage files, so delete the one available at the root project level. Since we moved the location of the starting MainPage under the View folder, in order to run the project successfully you need to visit the app.xaml.cs file and change starting page from MainPage to FinanceHub.View.MainPage as shown below.

```
var rootFrame = new Frame();
if (!rootFrame.Navigate(typeof(FinanceHub.View.MainPage)))
{
    throw new Exception("Failed to create initial page");
}
```

Now if you run the project it should locate the blank MainPage as a starting page and will run successfully.

Adding Bottom Application Bar – MainPage.xaml

Microsoft introduced the Application Bar (AKA app bar) UI element to the Windows 8 application that typically appears at the top and/or bottom of the screen. Typically the top app bar represents navigation and the bottom app bar represents commands and tools related to the application. App Bar is not mandatory to the application and if you want you can define either top or bottom or both app bars. By default it is not visible and you can invoke it (make it visible) by right-clicking, pressing Windows + Z or by swiping from the bottom or top of the screen.

The AppBar user control can contain one or more application UI controls to create the navigation, commands, and tool bar. In XAML you can add AppBar control as a top app bar by assigning it to the TopAppBar property of Page and add bottom app bar by assigning AppBar control to the BottomAppBar property of Page control.

For FinanceHub application, we will have the bottom app bar, which will be available to all pages of the application, containing commands to add and remove stock watch list. Add the following to `MainPage.xaml` file.

```xml
<!--Bottom Application bar-->
<Page.BottomAppBar>
    <AppBar x:Name="BottomAppBar1" Padding="10,0,10,0">

    </AppBar>
</Page.BottomAppBar>
```

Next add two buttons – Add and Remove – in the bottom app bar as shown below.

```xml
<Page.BottomAppBar>
    <AppBar x:Name="BottomAppBar1" Padding="10,0,10,0">
        <Grid>
            <Grid.ColumnDefinitions>
                <ColumnDefinition Width="50*"/>
                <ColumnDefinition Width="50*"/>
            </Grid.ColumnDefinitions>

            <StackPanel
                x:Name="RightPanel" Orientation="Horizontal"
                Grid.Column="1" HorizontalAlignment="Right">
                <Button x:Name="Remove" BorderBrush="{x:Null}"
                    Click="RemoveStock">
                    <Button.ContentTemplate>
                        <DataTemplate>
                            <StackPanel>
                                <Image
                                    Source="../Assets/minus.png"
                                    Height="48" Width="48"/>
                                <TextBlock Text="Remove"
                                    HorizontalAlignment="Center" >
                                </TextBlock>
                            </StackPanel>
                        </DataTemplate>
                    </Button.ContentTemplate>
                </Button>
                <Button x:Name="Add" Content="Add"
                    BorderBrush="{x:Null}"
                    Click="AddNewStock">
                    <Button.ContentTemplate>
                        <DataTemplate>
                            <StackPanel>
                                <Image Source="../Assets/add.png"
                                    Height="48" Width="48"/>
                                <TextBlock Text="Add"
                                    HorizontalAlignment="Center" >
                                </TextBlock>
                            </StackPanel>
```

```
            </DataTemplate>
          </Button.ContentTemplate>
        </Button>
      </StackPanel>
    </Grid>
  </AppBar>
</Page.BottomAppBar>
```

Two main things to note. First you will see a reference to two image files – minus.png and add.png – under the Assets folder. Please add these two files (provided as part of the source code with your purchase of this book) to display them as Remove and Add buttons respectively.

Second you will notice that each button – Add and Remove – has a Click event associated with it. To create a Click event handler for Add and Remove buttons named AddNewStock and RemoveStock respectively, right-click on the event handler name and select navigate to event handler so Visual Studio will add the code-behind for the events, which you can confirm by visiting the MainPage.xaml.cs file.

If you run the project at this point and swipe at the bottom or top of the screen edge you should see a bottom app bar displaying right aligned Add and Remove buttons as shown in Figure 2-4. However, if you click or tap on those buttons nothing will happen since we have not implemented the business logic yet.

Figure 2-4. FinanceHub Application with Bottom Application Bar

---

▨ **Note** Visual Studio 2012 has a Windows 8 application simulator where you can experiment with common touch and rotate events. To run and debug application in the Simulator mode you should select Simulator from the drop-down list next to the Start Debugging button on the debugger Standard toolbar in Visual Studio 2012. You can get more details on this by visiting MSDN site – `http://msdn.microsoft.com/en-us/library/hh441475.aspx`.

As discussed earlier `MainPage.xaml` is a master navigation page that contains the bottom app bar and this page needs to be visible all the time throughout the application. You can achieve this by defining a `Frame` named `mainPageFrame` within the `MainPage.xaml` file as shown below. We will set this frame as the main frame for navigation, keeping `Mainpage` in view all the time and providing navigation to different application pages using this frame.

```
<Grid
    Background="{StaticResource
    ApplicationPageBackgroundThemeBrush}"
    Style="{StaticResource LayoutRootStyle}">
    <Frame x:Name="mainPageFrame"/>
</Grid>
```

Also we will be developing a `NavigationService` at a later stage to separate the presentation and business logic following MVVM design pattern. In order to implement that in the future let's expose this `mainPageFrame` frame as a property by adding the following code in the `MainPage.xaml.cs` code-behind.

```
/// Application wide Frame control to be used
///in Navigation Service
public Frame AppFrame
{
    get
    {
        return this.mainPageFrame;
    }
}
```

Setting Up Remaining Custom Resources and Styles in Resources.xaml

Before we further add other stock-related XAML pages let's add additional styles required to support development. For that, open `Resources.xaml` file and add the following custom resources to be used to display stock-related details.

```
<!--Custom resources-->
<SolidColorBrush x:Key="ApplicationTitleColorBrush"
    Color="{StaticResource AppLightPurpleColor}" />
```

```xml
<SolidColorBrush x:Key="StockTilesBackgroundBrush"
    Color="#f8f5f5"/>
<SolidColorBrush x:Key="StockDetailForegroundBrush"
    Color="DarkBlue" />
<SolidColorBrush x:Key="StockDetailLightBlueForegroundBrush"
    Color="#759CC8" />
<SolidColorBrush x:Key="StockChangePositiveForegroundBrush"
    Color="DarkGreen" />
<SolidColorBrush x:Key="StockChangeNegativeForegroundBrush"
    Color="DarkRed" />
<SolidColorBrush x:Key="StockCaptionBrush" Color="DarkGray" />
```

Next add the following styles: DetailTextStyle, CaptionTextStyle, and HeaderTextStyle that would drive the text styles in stock-related pages. Please notice that we will use two resources, as defined above, to determine the foreground color of the DetailTextStyle and HeaderTextStyle styles.

```xml
<!--Custom Styles -->
<Style x:Key="DetailTextStyle" TargetType="TextBlock" >
    <Setter Property="FontWeight" Value="SemiBold"/>
    <Setter Property="Foreground"
        Value="{StaticResource StockDetailForegroundBrush}"/>
    <Setter Property="FontSize" Value="22"/>
    <Setter Property="Margin" Value="5" />
</Style>

<Style x:Key="CaptionTextStyle" TargetType="TextBlock" >
    <Setter Property="FontWeight" Value="SemiBold"/>
    <Setter Property="Foreground" Value="White"/>
    <Setter Property="FontSize" Value="22"/>
    <Setter Property="Margin" Value="5" />
</Style>

<Style x:Key="HeaderTextStyle" TargetType="TextBlock"
    BasedOn="{StaticResource CaptionTextStyle}" >
    <Setter Property="Foreground"
        Value="{StaticResource ApplicationTitleColorBrush}"/>
    <Setter Property="FontSize" Value="26"/>
</Style>
```

Adding Stocks Page – StocksPage.xaml

We are going to follow a Hierarchical navigation pattern to build the FinanceHub application. The Hierarchical navigation pattern follows the Hub – Spoke – Details model, as shown in Figure 2-5. The Hierarchical pattern presents the Items (Hub), Sub items or first-level details (Spoke), and further content details (Details).

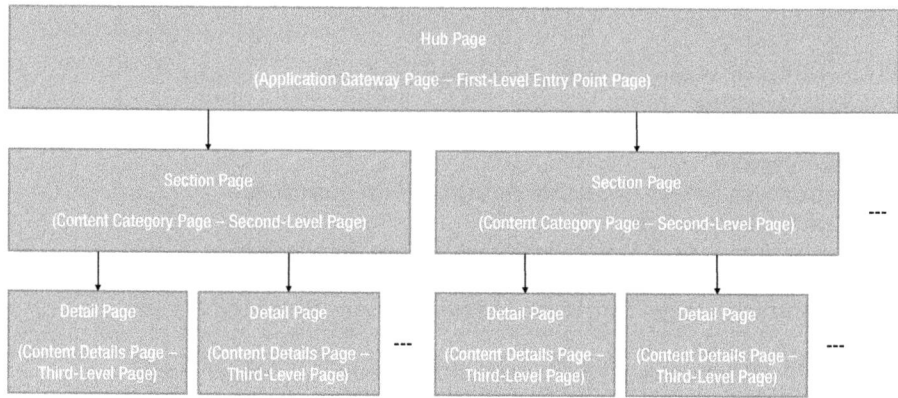

Figure 2-5. *Hierarchical Navigation Pattern for Windows 8 Applications*

For simplicity and to maintain our focus on implementation of MVVM and not developing full commercial application, this book will implement Hub (List of Stocks) and Spoke (Details of Stock) only. This section covers the user interface implementation of the Hub – the Stock page, which will list a set of stocks added to your watch list and each stock will be represented as an individual tile.

Windows 8 comes up with a set of XAML page templates to build Windows 8 applications easily and follow design principles of Windows 8 application user interface consistently across application. One of the available templates is an Item Page template, which displays a collection of items. This template is suitable to display stocks to our application. Add a stock page named StocksPage.xaml of type Item Page under the View folder.

When you add an Item type page for the first time in your project you should be receiving a pop-up message as shown in Figure 2-6 asking permission to add required dependency files under Common folder automatically. Please make sure you click the Yes button to add these required files automatically; otherwise you have to add/code them manually.

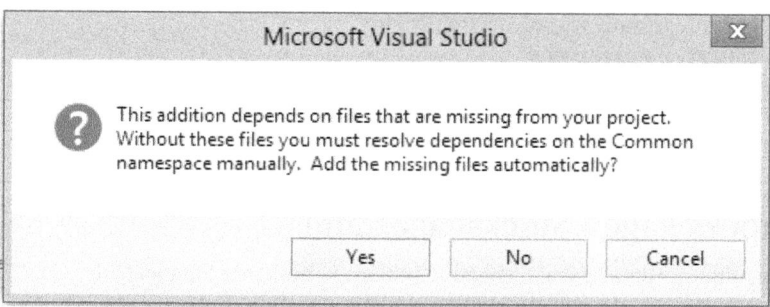

Figure 2-6. *Getting Permission to Add Required Dependencies Files while Adding an Item Page*

You will notice that 6 utility classes and ReadMe.txt files are added (shown in Figure 2-7) as dependency classes under Common folder.

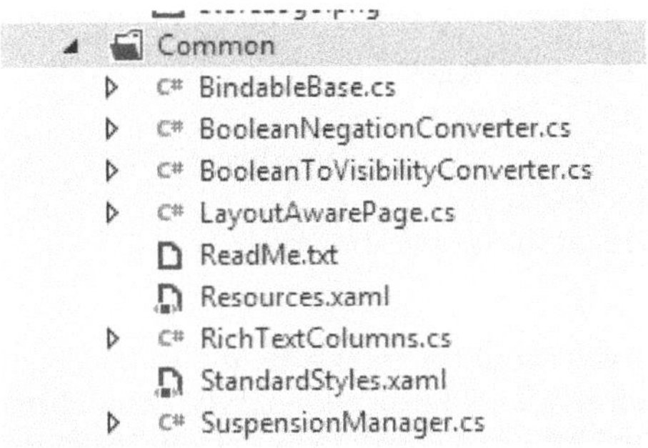

Figure 2-7. *Automatically Added 6 Utility Classed Under Common Folder*

Set Application Name

We need to display the application name across the application and thus we need to move the string resource named AppName from its default location StocksPage.xaml file to the App.xaml file, making it an application-level resource rather than just a page-specific resource.

To implement this first, open StocksPage.xaml file and delete the following line of code that declares the key AppName under Page.Resources, since we will declare it in the App.xaml file.

```
<!-- TODO: Delete this line if the key AppName is declared in App.xaml -->
<x:String x:Key="AppName">My Application</x:String>
```

Now open App.xaml file and declare key AppName under ResourceDictionary that will be used to display the application name – Finance Hub – in the application.

```
<ResourceDictionary>
    . . .

    <x:String x:Key="AppName">Finance Hub</x:String>
</ResourceDictionary>
```

You will notice in the design view of the StocksPage.xaml that the application name has changed from My Application to Finance Hub as page title in the page header section of the page.

Display Application Logo with Application Name

In order to display an application logo with the application name you need to change the existing code a little bit. Before changing the code first visit the Assets folder and add AppLogo.png image file, which will be used to display the application logo.

Now open StocksPage.xaml file and add the horizontal oriented StackPanel that will contain the application logo as shown below.

```
<StackPanel Orientation="Horizontal" Grid.Column="1" Margin="90,0,0,0">
    <Image
        Source="../Assets/AppLogo.png" Stretch="None"
        Height="80" Width="80" Margin="10" ></Image>
    <TextBlock x:Name="pageTitle"  Text="{StaticResource AppName}"
        Style="{StaticResource PageHeaderTextStyle}"
        Foreground="{StaticResource ApplicationTitleColorBrush}"/>
</StackPanel>
```

At this point if you look at the design view, you should be seeing the application logo and application name. At runtime the back button will not be displayed if you do not have multiple pages but it will keep the space required by the back button by default. To adjust this you need to set the Visibility property of the back button to Collapsed. Revisit StocksPage.xaml and make the appropriate modifications as shown below.

```
<Button x:Name="backButton" Visibility="Collapsed" Click="GoBack"
    IsEnabled="{Binding Frame.CanGoBack, ElementName=pageRoot}"
    Style="{StaticResource BackButtonStyle}"/>
```

Now you will notice that the back button is not displayed and the space is adjusted properly.

Finally add StocksPage.xaml page as a navigation page to be displayed in the mainPageFrame to enable showing list of stocks as a startup page. For this revisit MainPage.xaml.cs file and add the following in the existing OnNavigateTo event.

```
/// Invoked when this page is about to be displayed in a Frame.
protected override void OnNavigatedTo(NavigationEventArgs e)
{
    this.mainPageFrame.Navigate(typeof(StocksPage));
}
```

Display One Stock for Demonstration Purpose

Open StocksPage.xaml.cs file and first you need to add Stock class as shown below that would maintain the hard-coded stock information – stock symbol, open price, change in price, and current price.

```
#region Stock class
public class Stock
{
    public string Symbol { get; set; }
    public decimal OpenPrice { get; set; }
    public decimal Change { get; set; }
    public decimal CurrentPrice { get; set; }
}
#endregion
```

As you probably know, in XAML the DataTemplate class enables structuring custom and rich visual representation of the data by defining rendering of data object as a template. Before we start adding the remaining code to display the stocks first you need to create a DataTemplate with the name StockTilesTemplate in the Resources.xaml file that will control the visual representation of the stock information to be displayed on stock tiles. You would bind the above created Stock class attributes and display them appropriately within a stock tile.

```
<DataTemplate x:Key="StockTilesTemplate">
    <Border BorderBrush="{StaticResource AppBarBorderThemeBrush}"
        BorderThickness="2">
        <Grid Background="{StaticResource
            StockTilesBackgroundBrush}"
            Height="155" Width="220">
            <TextBlock
                Foreground=
                    "{StaticResource StockDetailForegroundBrush}"
                HorizontalAlignment="Left"
                TextWrapping="Wrap" Text="{Binding Symbol}"
                VerticalAlignment="Top"
                Margin="10,10,0,0" Height="32" Width="200"
                    FontSize="24" />
            <TextBlock HorizontalAlignment="Left"
                TextWrapping="Wrap"
                Text="{Binding CurrentPrice}"
                VerticalAlignment="Top" Margin="60,96,0,0"
                Height="51" Width="151" FontSize="42"
                Foreground="{StaticResource
                    StockDetailLightBlueForegroundBrush}" />
            <Path Data="M211,23" Fill="#FFBF2B00"
                HorizontalAlignment="Left" Height="0"
                Margin="211,23,0,0" Stretch="Fill"
                UseLayoutRounding="False"
                VerticalAlignment="Top"
                Width="0"/>
            <Path Data="M141,31 L179,31 L160,56" Fill="#FFBF2B00"
                HorizontalAlignment="Left"
                Height="18.092" Margin="10,113.908,0,0"
                Stretch="Fill" UseLayoutRounding="False"
                VerticalAlignment="Top" Width="27.5"
                Visibility="Collapsed"/>
            <Path Data="M141,31 L179,31 L160,56" Fill="#FF108104"
                HorizontalAlignment="Left"
                Height="18.092" Margin="10,120.908,0,0"
                Stretch="Fill" UseLayoutRounding="False"
                VerticalAlignment="Top" Width="27.5"
                RenderTransformOrigin="0.5,0.5">
```

```
                <Path.RenderTransform>
                    <CompositeTransform Rotation="180"/>
                </Path.RenderTransform>
            </Path>
            <TextBlock HorizontalAlignment="Left"
                TextWrapping="Wrap" Text="Open"
                VerticalAlignment="Top" Margin="10.5,47,0,0"
                FontSize="18.667"
                 Foreground="DarkGray"/>
            <TextBlock HorizontalAlignment="Left"
                TextWrapping="Wrap"
                Text="{Binding OpenPrice}"
                VerticalAlignment="Top" Margin="98.5,47,0,0"
                FontSize="18.667"
                Foreground="#6a7bba" Width="111.5"/>
            <TextBlock HorizontalAlignment="Left"
                TextWrapping="Wrap" Text="Change"
                VerticalAlignment="Top" Margin="10.5,74,0,0"
                Foreground="{StaticResource StockCaptionBrush}"
                FontSize="18.667"
                RenderTransformOrigin=
                    "0.666999995708466,0.455000013113022"/>
            <TextBlock HorizontalAlignment="Left"
                TextWrapping="Wrap" Text="{Binding Change}"
                VerticalAlignment="Top" Margin="98.5,74,0,0"
                FontSize="18.667"
                Foreground="{StaticResource
                    StockChangePositiveForegroundBrush}"
                Width="111.5"/>
        </Grid>
    </Border>
</DataTemplate>
```

Now revisit the `itemGridView` GridView control in the `StocksPage.xaml` file and set the `SelectionMode` property to None to disable the selection and `ItemTemplate` to the `StockTilesTemplate` data template we just created above to display each item. The related code snippet is shown below.

```
<GridView
    x:Name="itemGridView"
    AutomationProperties.AutomationId="ItemsGridView"
    AutomationProperties.Name="Items"
    SelectionMode="None"
    TabIndex="1"
    Grid.Row="1"
    Margin="0,-4,0,0"
```

```
Padding="116,0,116,46"
ItemsSource=
    "{Binding Source={StaticResource itemsViewSource}}"
ItemTemplate="{StaticResource StockTilesTemplate}"/>
```

Make similar changes to the itemListView ListView control.

```
<ListView
    . . . .
SelectionMode="None"
    . . . .
ItemTemplate="{StaticResource StockTilesTemplate}"/>
```

Next just to display one stock for demonstration purposes we will hardcode one stock – MSFT – in the StocksPage.xaml code-behind. However, we will remove it and create clear separate View layer in later chapters. We will use ObservableCollection holding the stock price. For that, first you need to add reference to the System.Collections.ObjectModel as shown below in StocksPage.xaml.cs file.

```
using System.Collections.ObjectModel;
```

Next visit the LoadState method of this page and add MSFT stock related information to the ObservableCollection and assign this collection to DefaultViewModel's Items key as shown below.

```
protected override void LoadState(Object navigationParameter,
    Dictionary<String, Object> pageState)
{
    var collection = new ObservableCollection<Stock>();
    collection.Add(new Stock
    { Symbol = "MSFT",
      OpenPrice = 30.05M,
      Change = 0.25M,
      CurrentPrice = 30.30M
    });
    this.DefaultViewModel["Items"] = collection;
}
```

Run the application in the simulation mode and you will see the application logo and application name in the application header section and MSFT stock tile with appropriate stock information displayed as shown in Figure 2-8.

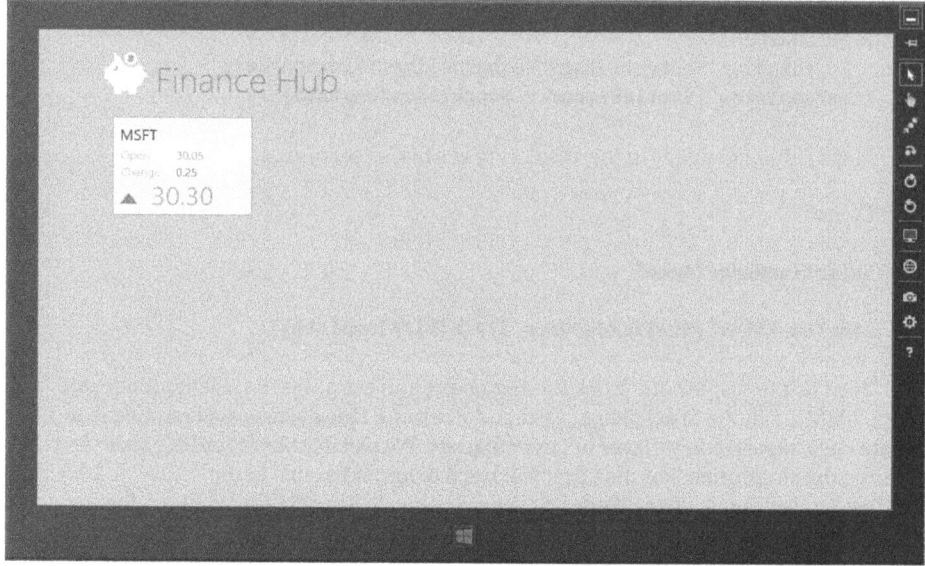

Figure 2-8. FinanceHub Application Running with the Main Page displaying Stock Tile

Adding Stock Details Page – StockInfoView.xaml and StockDetails.xaml

If you click on the MSFT stock tile nothing will happen. Next, navigate to the implement stock details page by clicking on the stock tile, which will display a bit more information related to the clicked stock. In this chapter we will focus on building the stock detail user interface and enabling the navigation to this page. We will worry about how to bind data from the data source in later chapters.

The stock details page contains lists of stocks and will display the selected stock information in a split view. So first let's create a view that will display selected stock information and then will create the stock details page and plug-in the stock information view to it, building complete user interface.

Adding StockInfoView.xaml User Control

Select View folder in the Solution Explorer and add a new blank UserControl type template with the name StockInfoView.xaml. The following is the default XAML code of the added user control.

```
<UserControl
    x:Class="FinanceHub.View.StockInfoView"
    xmlns=
        "http://schemas.microsoft.com/winfx/2006/xaml/presentation"
    xmlns:x="http://schemas.microsoft.com/winfx/2006/xaml"
```

```xml
        xmlns:local="using:FinanceHub.View"
        xmlns:d="http://schemas.microsoft.com/expression/blend/2008"
        xmlns:mc=
         "http://schemas.openxmlformats.org/markup-compatibility/2006"
        mc:Ignorable="d"
        d:DesignHeight="300"
        d:DesignWidth="400">

        <Grid>

        </Grid>
</UserControl>
```

Now remove the existing Grid control and let's add required UI elements within StackPanel as shown in the following code snippet that will display the following information with Stock Details title text and related hard-coded values (for this chapter only):

- Current Price

- Open Price

- Today High and Low Range

- 52 Weeks High and Low Range

```xml
<StackPanel>
    <TextBlock Text="Stock Details"
        Style="{StaticResource HeaderTextStyle}" Margin="5" />
    <TextBlock
        Text="Current Price"
        Style="{StaticResource CaptionTextStyle}" Margin="5"/>
    <TextBlock
        Style="{StaticResource DetailTextStyle}"
        Text="30.30"/>
    <TextBlock
        Text="Open Price"
        Style="{StaticResource CaptionTextStyle}" Margin="5"/>
    <TextBlock
        Style="{StaticResource DetailTextStyle}"
        Text="30.05"/>
    <TextBlock
        Text="Today High and Low Range"
        Style="{StaticResource CaptionTextStyle}" Margin="5"/>
    <TextBlock
        Style="{StaticResource DetailTextStyle}"
        Text="30.33 - 30.05"/>
    <TextBlock
        Text="52 Weeks High and Low Range"
        Style="{StaticResource CaptionTextStyle}" Margin="5"/>
```

```
    <TextBlock
        Style="{StaticResource DetailTextStyle}"
        Text="32.95 - 24.26"/>
</StackPanel>
```

If you look at the design view you should see the user interface of the user control as shown in Figure 2-9.

Figure 2-9. *Design View of the StockInfoView.xaml UserControl*

Please note that in a real-world application you probably would like to put more information in the stock details page.

Adding StockDetails.xaml Split Page

Again select View folder in the solution explorer and add a new Split Page template with the name StockDetails.xaml, which will display a list of items (in our case list of stocks) and the details for a selected item (in our case StockInfoView of the selected stock).

Open StocksDetails.xaml page and locate the TextBlock control with the name set to pageTitle and set Text property to AppName value as shown below.

```
<TextBlock x:Name="pageTitle" Grid.Column="1"
    Text="{Binding Group.Title}" Text="{StaticResource AppName}"
    Style="{StaticResource PageHeaderTextStyle}
    Foreground="{StaticResource ApplicationTitleColorBrush}"/>
```

Next locate primaryColumn ColumnDefinition and change the Width from 610 to 400 as shown below.

```
<Grid.ColumnDefinitions>
    <ColumnDefinition x:Name="primaryColumn" Width="400"/>
    <ColumnDefinition Width="*"/>
</Grid.ColumnDefinitions>
```

Now we have to make two key changes in the XAML code first to bind the list view with the stock information and second to plug in the stock information detail view to display the selected stock details.

In order to view the list of stocks; first you need to add a DataTemplate with the name StockListTemplate in Resources.xaml file similar to the one you added earlier for StocksPage.xaml.

```
<DataTemplate x:Key="StockListTemplate">
    <Border BorderBrush="{StaticResource AppBarBorderThemeBrush}"
        BorderThickness="2">
        <Grid Background="#f8f5f5"  Height="110" Width="220">
            <TextBlock Foreground="{StaticResource
                                    StockDetailForegroundBrush}"
                HorizontalAlignment="Left" TextWrapping="Wrap"
                Text="{Binding Symbol}"
                VerticalAlignment="Top" Margin="10,10,0,0"
                Height="32" Width="200"
                 FontSize="24" />
            <Path Data="M211,23" Fill="#FFBF2B00"
                HorizontalAlignment="Left" Height="0"
                Margin="211,23,0,0" Stretch="Fill"
                UseLayoutRounding="False"
                VerticalAlignment="Top"
                Width="0"/>
            <Path Data="M141,31 L179,31 L160,56"
                Fill="#FFBF2B00" HorizontalAlignment="Left"
                Height="18.092" Margin="10,113.908,0,0"
                Stretch="Fill" UseLayoutRounding="False"
                VerticalAlignment="Top" Width="27.5"
                Visibility="Collapsed"/>
            <TextBlock HorizontalAlignment="Left"
                TextWrapping="Wrap" Text="Open"
                VerticalAlignment="Top" Margin="10.5,47,0,0"
                FontSize="18.667"
                Foreground="{StaticResource StockCaptionBrush}"/>
            <TextBlock HorizontalAlignment="Left"
                TextWrapping="Wrap"
                Text="{Binding OpenPrice}"
                VerticalAlignment="Top" Margin="98.5,47,0,0"
                FontSize="18.667"
                Foreground="{StaticResource
                            StockDetailLightBlueForegroundBrush}"
                Width="111.5"/>
```

```
            <TextBlock HorizontalAlignment="Left"
                TextWrapping="Wrap" Text="Change"
                VerticalAlignment="Top" Margin="10.5,74,0,0"
                Foreground="{StaticResource StockCaptionBrush}"
                FontSize="18.667"
                 RenderTransformOrigin=
                    "0.666999995708466,0.455000013113022"/>
            <TextBlock HorizontalAlignment="Left"
                TextWrapping="Wrap" Text="0.25%"
                VerticalAlignment="Top" Margin="98.5,74,0,0"
                FontSize="18.667"
                Foreground="{StaticResource
                                StockChangePositiveForegroundBrush}"
                Width="111.5"/>
        </Grid>
    </Border>
</DataTemplate>
```

Now revisit the itemListView ListView control in the StockDetails.xaml file and set the SelectionMode property to None to disable the selection and ItemTemplate to the StockListTemplate data template we just created above to display each item. The related code snippet is shown below.

```
<ListView
    x:Name="itemListView"
    AutomationProperties.AutomationId="ItemsListView"
    AutomationProperties.Name="Items"
    TabIndex="1"
    Grid.Row="1"
    SelectionMode="None"
    Margin="-10,-10,0,0"
    Padding="120,0,0,60"
    ItemsSource=
        "{Binding Source={StaticResource itemsViewSource}}"
    IsSwipeEnabled="False"
    SelectionChanged="ItemListView_SelectionChanged"
    ItemTemplate="{StaticResource StockListTemplate}"/>
```

Next, to add the user control StockInfoView to this page you first need to declare it as shown below:

```
<common:LayoutAwarePage
    x:Name="pageRoot"
    .....
    xmlns:control="using:FinanceHub.View"
    mc:Ignorable="d">
```

Now locate the itemDetail ScrollViewer control and remove the following code.

```
<Image Grid.Row="1" Margin="0,0,20,0" Width="180" Height="180"
    Source="{Binding Image}"
    Stretch="UniformToFill"/>
<StackPanel x:Name="itemDetailTitlePanel" Grid.Row="1"
    Grid.Column="1">
    <TextBlock x:Name="itemTitle" Margin="0,-10,0,0"
        Text="{Binding Title}"
        Style="{StaticResource SubheaderTextStyle}"/>
    <TextBlock x:Name="itemSubtitle" Margin="0,0,0,20"
        Text="{Binding Subtitle}"
        Style="{StaticResource TitleTextStyle}"/>
</StackPanel>
<TextBlock Grid.Row="2" Grid.ColumnSpan="2" Margin="0,20,0,0"
    Text="{Binding Content}"
    Style="{StaticResource BodyTextStyle}"/>
```

Finally add StockInfoView to the itemDetail ScrollViewer to display the selected stock details as shown below.

```
<control:StockInfoView Grid.Row="1"></control:StockInfoView>
```

At this point you are all set with the StockDetails.xaml page. Now open the code-behind StockDetails.xaml.cs page and visit the existing LoadState method of this page and add MSFT stock related information to the ObservableCollection and assign this collection to DefaultViewModel's Items key as shown below as we did for StocksPage.xaml.cs code-behind.

```
protected override void LoadState(Object navigationParameter,
Dictionary<String, Object> pageState)
{
    var collection = new ObservableCollection<Stock>();
    collection.Add(new Stock
    { Symbol = "MSFT",
      OpenPrice = 30.05M,
      Change = 0.25M,
      CurrentPrice = 30.30M
    });
    this.DefaultViewModel["Items"] = collection;

    ...
}
```

The remaining task is to implement a click event to the StocksPage so that upon clicking the stock from the StocksPage it navigates to the StockDetails page. In later chapters we will implement proper binding following MVVM design pattern.

Revisit StocksPage.xaml page itemGridView GridView control and set the IsItemClickEnabled attribute to True and set the ItemClick event to ClickedStock method as shown below.

```
<GridView
    x:Name="itemGridView"
    AutomationProperties.AutomationId="ItemsGridView"
    AutomationProperties.Name="Items"
    TabIndex="1"
    Grid.Row="1"
    SelectionMode ="None"
    IsItemClickEnabled="True"
    ItemClick="ClickedStock"
    Margin="0,-4,0,0"
    Padding="116,0,116,46"
    ItemsSource=
        "{Binding Source={StaticResource itemsViewSource}}"
    ItemTemplate="{StaticResource StockTilesTemplate}"/>
```

Make similar changes to itemListView ListView control.

```
<ListView
    ....
    IsItemClickEnabled="True"
    ItemClick="ClickedStock"
    ....
    />
```

Now open code-behind StocksPage.xaml.cs file and implement ClickStock event that basically navigates to the StockDetails page.

```
void ClickedStock(object sender, ItemClickEventArgs e)
{
    this.Frame.Navigate(typeof(StockDetails));
}
```

You are all set to build and run the project. You should be in a position to click on the MSFT tile and get the details page as shown in Figure 2-10. If you click on the Back button you will go back to the stock main page displaying MSFT stock tile.

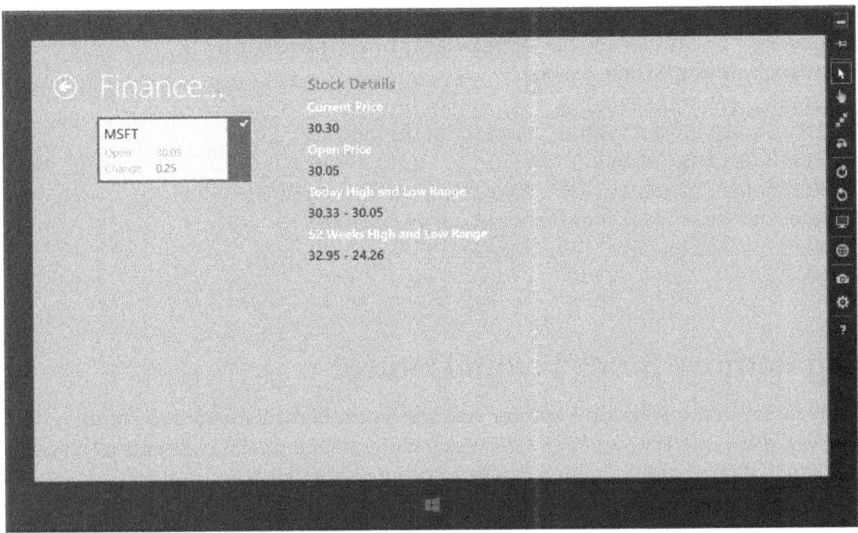

Figure 2-10. *Stock Details Page*

Adding Add Stock Flyout Control

There are only two remained items to build the final view are implementing Add and Remove stock flyout controls, which will be driven by the bottom app bar Add and Remove buttons.

■ **Note** Flyout controls provide traditional pop-up window functionality to Windows 8 applications. You usually display the content in the flyout control that you do not want to keep on the screen all the time. Even they are potentially used when you would like to implement pop-up window like user interface, you must follow guidelines of designing flyout controls to make your application qualified to be deployed in the Windows app store. You can get more details on this by visiting MSDN site – `http://msdn.microsoft.com/en-us/library/windows/apps/hh465341.aspx`.

Select `View` folder in the solution explorer and add a new blank `UserControl` type template with the name `AddStockView.xaml`. Remove the existing Grid control and instead add a StackPanel and add a caption, text box, and button that would allow the user to add a stock symbol to add it in the user's watch list. The following is a complete code snippet.

```
<StackPanel
    Background="{StaticResource AppBarBackgroundThemeBrush}">
    <TextBlock Text="Stock Symbol"
        Style="{StaticResource CaptionTextStyle}" Margin="5"/>
    <TextBox x:Name="txtSymbol" HorizontalAlignment="Left"
        TextWrapping="Wrap"
        VerticalAlignment="Top" Margin="5" Width="380"/>
    <Button Content="Add" HorizontalAlignment="Left"
        VerticalAlignment="Top" Margin="5"/>
</StackPanel>
```

Adding Remove Stock Flyout Control

Select View folder in the Solution Explorer and add a new blank UserControl type
template with the name RemoveStockView.xaml. Here we will put UI elements a ListView
control that will display stocks, which can be selected using CheckBox control, and a
button to remove selected one or more stocks:

```
<Grid Background="{StaticResource AppBarBackgroundThemeBrush}" >
    <Grid.RowDefinitions>
        <RowDefinition/>
        <RowDefinition Height="42"/>
    </Grid.RowDefinitions>
    <ListView
        Background="{StaticResource AppBarBackgroundThemeBrush}">
        <ListView.ItemTemplate>
            <DataTemplate>
                <CheckBox/>
            </DataTemplate>
        </ListView.ItemTemplate>
    </ListView>
    <Button Content="Remove Selected"
        HorizontalAlignment="Stretch"
        Grid.Row="1">
    </Button>
</Grid>
```

Integrating Flyout Controls with Bottom Application Bar

We will end the chapter by writing some C# code to integrate Add and Remove flyout
controls with the bottom app bar Add and Remove buttons click events.

Creating UIHelper Dependency Class

To perform this task, first we need to create a generic method that can handle displaying of the requested flyout control as pop-up and manage when to dismiss it. Windows 8 application should support both virtual keyboard for touch-enabled devices and physical keyboards. Let's get started.

First add a UIHelper class under the Common folder by selecting the folder and add a new empty class with the name UIHelper.cs.

Next add the following additional references to support our implementation.

```
using Windows.Foundation;
using Windows.UI.Xaml;
using Windows.UI.Xaml.Controls;
using Windows.UI.Xaml.Controls.Primitives;
using Windows.UI.Xaml.Media;
using Windows.UI.Xaml.Media.Animation;
```

Now we will create a new method named ShowPopup with FrameworkElement parameter to determine the position of the flyout to display and UserControl parameter that determines which control to display. As explained earlier this method performs three main functions:

1. Creates a new instance of the Popup class

2. Defines position of the pop-up instance, enables light dismiss by setting Popup.IsLightDismissEnabled property to true (this will dismiss the pop-up as soon as user taps or clicks to any other area outside of the pop-up) and display the pop-up

3. Handle virtual key board by using new event introduced in WinRT Windows.UI.ViewManagement.InputPane. GetForCurrentView().Showing

The following code snippet represents the ShowPopup method added to the UIHelper class.

```
public static Popup ShowPopup
    (FrameworkElement source, UserControl control)
{
    Popup flyout = new Popup();

    var windowBounds = Window.Current.Bounds;
    var rootVisual = Window.Current.Content;

    //Define Flyout Control Position,
    //Enable Light Dismiss and Display Popup
    GeneralTransform gt = source.TransformToVisual(rootVisual);

    var absolutePosition = gt.TransformPoint(new Point(0, 0));
```

```
control.Measure(new
    Size(Double.PositiveInfinity, double.PositiveInfinity));

flyout.VerticalOffset =
    windowBounds.Height - control.Height - 120;
flyout.HorizontalOffset = (absolutePosition.X +
    source.ActualWidth / 2) - control.Width / 2;
flyout.IsLightDismissEnabled = true;

flyout.Child = control;
var transitions = new TransitionCollection();
transitions.Add(new PopupThemeTransition()
    { FromHorizontalOffset = 0, FromVerticalOffset = 100 });
flyout.ChildTransitions = transitions;
flyout.IsOpen = true;

// Handling the virtual keyboard
int flyoutOffset = 0;
Windows.UI.ViewManagement.InputPane.GetForCurrentView().
    Showing += (s, args) =>
{
    flyoutOffset = (int)args.OccludedRect.Height;
    flyout.VerticalOffset -= flyoutOffset;
};

Windows.UI.ViewManagement.InputPane.GetForCurrentView().
    Hiding += (s, args) =>
{
    flyout.VerticalOffset += flyoutOffset;
};

    return flyout;
}
```

■ **Note** The credit for the above code of the ShowPopup method goes to author David Catuhe, who has blogged how to display flyout controls as a pop-up and handle virtual keyboard on the MSDN blog. For more details, visit http://blogs.msdn.com/b/eternalcoding/archive/ 2012/07/09/tips-and-tricks-for-c-metro-developers-handling-the-virtual- keyboard.aspx and http://blogs.msdn.com/b/eternalcoding/archive/2012/07/03/ tips-and-tricks-for-c-metro-developers-the-flyout-control.aspx links.

Implementing Buttons Click Events to Display Pop-up

Finally it's time to implement Click events for AddNewStock for the Add button and RemoveStock for the Remove button that we created with no business logic earlier in the chapter. Revisit MainPage.xaml.cs page and locate AddNewStock method.

First add the following three additional references to the code-behind to support our implementation.

```
using Windows.UI.Core;
using FinanceHub.Common;
using FinanceHub.View;
```

You can call CoreDispatcher.RunAsync on XAML UI element to run the event dispatcher and run as a task using the AsTask method that will return the results of the dispatched event asynchronously. For FinanceHub project we will call the UIHelper class ShowPopup method as an asynchronous operation as part of the Add and Remove button click events as shown below to display the related flyout controls. The following code snippet represents implementation of the Click events.

```
private void AddNewStock(object sender, RoutedEventArgs e)
{
    Dispatcher.RunAsync
        (CoreDispatcherPriority.Normal, new DispatchedHandler(() =>
        {
            UIHelper.ShowPopup(this, new AddStockView());
        })).AsTask();
}

private void RemoveStock(object sender, RoutedEventArgs e)
{
    Dispatcher.RunAsync
        (CoreDispatcherPriority.Normal, new DispatchedHandler(() =>
        {
            UIHelper.ShowPopup(this, new RemoveStockView());
        })).AsTask();
}
```

We have successfully completed the implementation of the View for the FinanceHub application. Now if you build your project and run it in the simulation mode you will see the project working as described earlier in this chapter including the bottom app bar with the functional add button (see Figure 2-11) and remove button (see Figure 2-12). You should also notice that the bottom app bar is available in both pages – stocks and stock details pages.

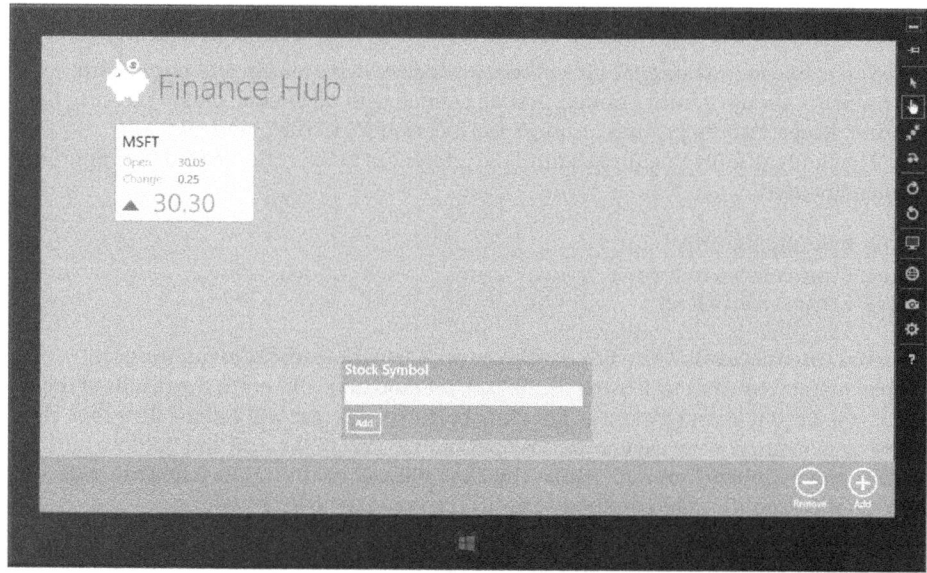

Figure 2-11. *Bottom App Bar with Functional Add Stock Button*

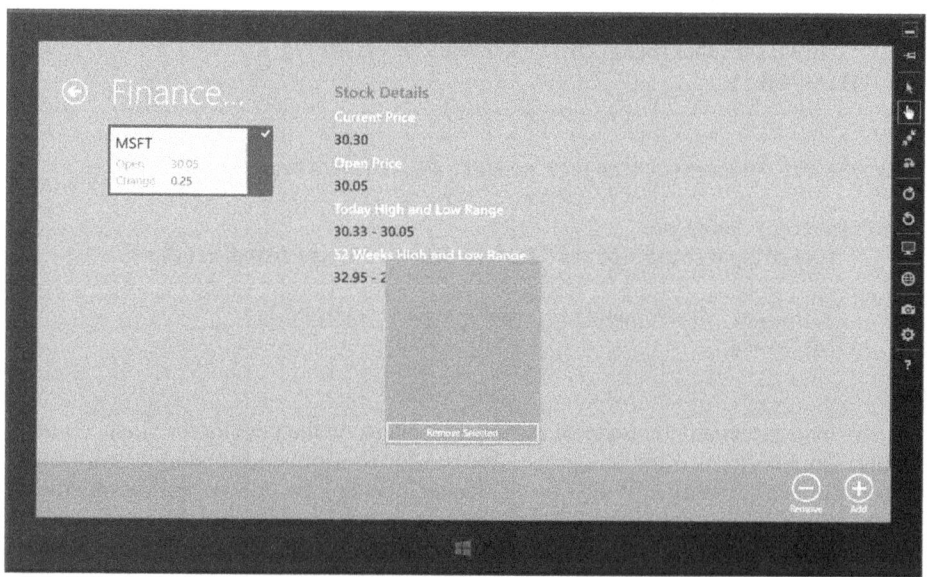

Figure 2-12. *Bottom App Bar with Functional Remove Stock Button*

Figure 2-13 shows the virtual keyboard enabling entry of the stock symbol in add stock flyout control.

Figure 2-13. *Virtual Key Board Enabled for the Data Entry*

Summary

We built Windows 8 application user interface following the hierarchical navigation pattern for the FinanceHub application. Along with building the user interface, we explored some of the key enhancements made in the XAML, such as use of `using` keyword to decorate the namespace in XAML and handling asynchronous operations as tasks, as well as some of the new properties introduced in WinRT. Visual Studio 2012 provides a simulator for debugging that would help test the different types of user interactions and different layout orientation models of the application.

Please note that we have hard-coded some values with the View definition for the complete end-to-end application demonstration purpose in this chapter. In the next two chapters we will remove the hard-coded value with the ViewModel and Model implementation separating out the View definition with the business logic and data source.

The next chapter defines the ViewModel of the application.

Do not forget to download the source code. Visit the `Chapter2` folder to view the source code that we developed in this chapter.

CHAPTER 3

Implementing the Model

When I started writing this book, I took some time before determining the current order of chapters 2, 3 and 4. There is always a great debate for MVVM implementation about what you design and implement first; Model, View or ViewModel? Theoretically if you look at the core of the Model-View-ViewModel design pattern, ViewModel is at the heart of the design implementation. It ties one or more Views (user interface) with the Model (your data source) by exposing properties on the Model objects and binding it to the Views. This would enable displaying the data as information as part of the application user interface. After giving it a lot of thought, I settled on the current sequence of the chapters, in which we first defined Views in the previous chapter, giving you a visual context; now we will define a lightweight model that determines the data source and required properties; and finally, in next chapter, we will implement ViewModels which will bind the model objects to the Views.

By definition, the model classes provide encapsulation of the application data and related business logic, providing maximum data integrity and data consistency. Basically it would implement application data model, integrate with the data sources, and implement required business logic for data retrieval and validation in order to provide data integrity and data consistency.

In this chapter we will create lightweight Model classes that essentially will implement the following items:

- Define serializable and deserializable stocks data model

- Define enum to support Add and Remove stocks actions

- Define a class for event arguments that will be passed as part of the Add and Remove stocks actions

- Create a helper class to store and retrieve stock watchlist in the local data storage

- Add stock details data file that would be used to simulate the "live" data update as you are integrating with live stock information service providers such as Microsoft Bing or Google or Yahoo

Define Serializable and Deserializable Stocks Data Model

In Chapter 2, we built a stocks details view in which you display all stock related information, as shown in Figure 3-1.

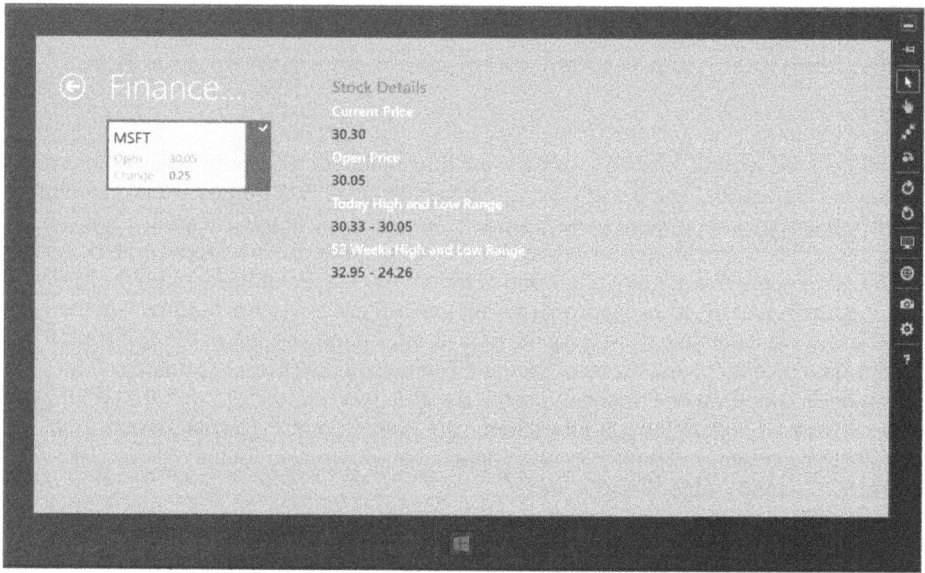

Figure 3-1. *StockDetails Page View Detailing Required Stocks Data Properties*

The stocks data model requires a data model that, at minimum, implements a class supporting the properties to support above displayed stock details (in Figure 3-1). To achieve this, we will create a *Stock* class with the required data properties as class members.

Open the project you finished in Chapter 2, and select the *Model* folder that we created as part of the creating of a skeleton of MVVM-based implementation in Chapter 1. Right click on the selected *Model* folder, and select Add Item option to add a new class. In the opened Add New Item window, select Class option, and name the class to *Stock.cs*, as shown in Figure 3-2, Click Add button to add a blank *Stock.cs* class under *Model* folder.

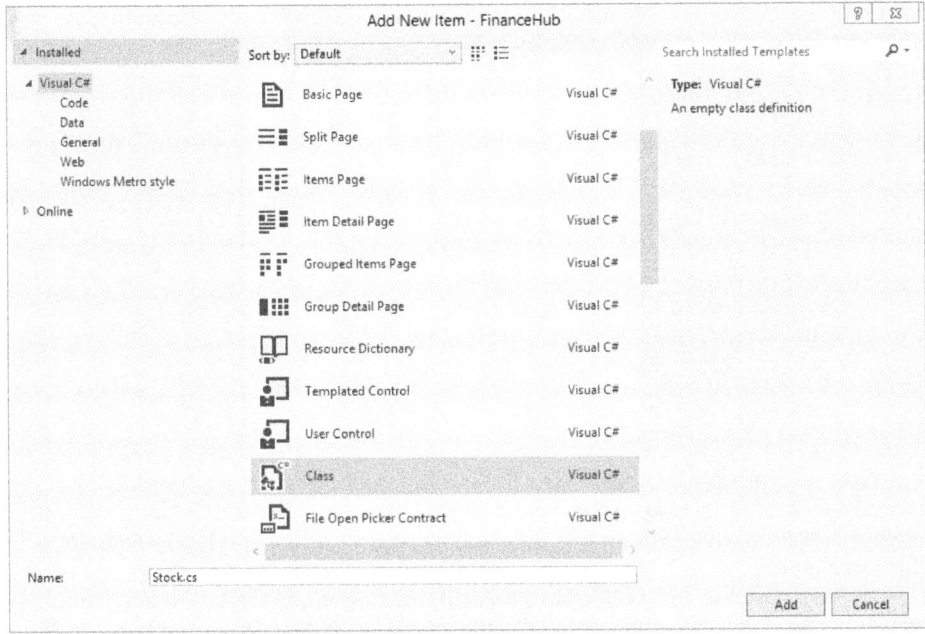

Figure 3-2. *Adding Stock.cs File*

Revisit Figure 3-1 and you will notice that you would need at least the following six information about the stock:

- Stock symbol (e.g. MSFT)

- Stock current price (e.g. 30.30)

- Stock open price (e.g. 30.05)

- Today's change in the stock prices - positive or negative value (e.g. +0.25)

- Range - Today's High and Low Price (e.g. 30.33 - 30.05)

- Range - 52 weeks High and Low Price (e.g. 32.95 - 24.26)

If you recall, in Chapter 2 we created a *Stock* class within the StocksPage.xaml.cs file that helped us to display the above mentioned stock-related information. We need to create a similar class as part of the Model to integrate it with the ViewModel in the next chapter. Create a new *Stock* class object containing these properties—Symbol,

CurrentPrice, OpenPrice, Change, DaysRange and Range52Week—incorporating the above mentioned information as shown below:

```
namespace FinanceHub.Model
{
    public class Stock
    {
        public string Symbol { get; set; }
        public decimal CurrentPrice { get; set; }
        public decimal OpenPrice { get; set; }
        public double Change { get; set; }
        public string DaysRange { get; set; }
        public string Range52Week { get; set; }
    }
}
```

Note that we are still going to keep the existing *Stock* class definition within the *StocksPage.xaml.cs* file to keep the current version of the application functional. We will remove it and start using the above implemented class when we develop ViewModel in the next chapter.

We will be saving the application stocks information to local storage as an offline state by using serialization and deserialization of the *Stock* class object. Let's update the above class so that it can be serialized/deserialized.

First add a reference to the *System.Runtime.Serialization* namespace (as shown below) that contains classes that can be used for the serialization and deserialization of the objects.

```
using System.Runtime.Serialization;
```

Next we will use the *KnownTypeAttributeClass* to specify the *Stock* class object type to be recognized by the *DataContractSerializer* class for the serialization and deserialization.

```
[KnownType(typeof(FinanceHub.Model.Stock))]
```

Finally, decoreate the *Stock* class with the *DataContractAttribute* class to make the class serializable, and deserializable as well, and decorate each *Stock* class members with the *DataMember* class to make every attribute as part of the data contract during serializing and deserializing.

The full revised code snippet of the *Stock* class is shown below:

```
using System.Runtime.Serialization;

namespace FinanceHub.Model
{
    [KnownType(typeof(FinanceHub.Model.Stock))]
    [DataContractAttribute]
    public class Stock
```

```
{
    [DataMember()]
    public string Symbol { get; set; }
    [DataMember()]
    public decimal CurrentPrice { get; set; }
    [DataMember()]
    public decimal OpenPrice { get; set; }
    [DataMember()]
    public double Change { get; set; }
    [DataMember()]
    public string DaysRange { get; set; }
    [DataMember()]
    public string Range52Week { get; set; }
    }
}
```

Define enum to support Add and Remove Stocks Actions

This application contains two actions—Add stock and Remove stock—that will be implemented using the pub-sub model by implementing *EventAggregator* class during the implementation of ViewModel in the next chapter, Chapter 4. To support that, we will be declaring *StockAction* enumeration as part of the Model implementation in this section.

Again select and right click on the Model folder, and select Add Item option to add a new class. In the opened Add New Item window, select Class option, name the class to *Enum.cs,* and click Add button to add a blank *Enum.cs* class under Model folder.

Now add *StockAction* enumeration with the enumerators *None, Add* and *Remove,* as shown below:

```
namespace FinanceHub.Model
{
    public enum StockAction
    {
        None,
        Add,
        Remove
    }
}
```

Define a Class for Event Arguments of Add and Remove Stocks Actions

Later in Chapter 4 we will be passing the above defined StockAction enum as an argument to implement stock add and remove actions. Add an additional class named

ActionEventArgs for event arguments, which will be passed as part of the Add and Remove stocks actions.

Again select and right click on the Model folder and select Add Item option to add a new class. In the opened Add New Item window, select Class option and name the class to *ActionEventArgs.cs*. Click Add button to add a blank *ActionEventArgs.cs* class under Model folder.

Add the following members to the *ActionEventArgs* class so when we publish message using *EventAggregator.Publish* method (to be defined in the next chapter 4), we will be passing an instance of the *ActionEventArgs* class with proper value for Data (new stock in the case of Add Stock action or stocks to be deleted in the case of Remove Stock action), with *StockAction* set to proper value.

```
namespace FinanceHub.Model
{
    public class ActionEventArgs
    {
        public StockAction Action { get; set; }
        public object Data { get; set; }
    }
}
```

Create a Helper Class to Store and Retrieve Stocks Watchlist in the Local Data Storage

Now let's prepare our application with offline capabilities, which we will be using to save the application state upon its suspension. For that we will store stocks information to the local storage using asynchronized serialization and deserialization process.

Before we actually implement this helper class, first let's get a quick overview of some of the new features related to handling asynchronous operations introduced in .NET Framework 4.5 and new class and APIs introduced with WinRT to support local storage capabilities.

Asynchronous Operations and Local Storage Capabilities for Windows 8 Applications

Microsoft .NET Framework 4.5 version established a very simplified, brand-new way of implementing the asynchronous operations, compared to the traditional legacy approach that uses callbacks.

The async Modifier and await Operator

Now, to define an asynchronous method to perform asynchronous operation, you need to define a method that ends with "Async" keyword, and you decorate the method with the async modifier. This method must contain at least one statement/expression that starts with the await operator. This method runs synchronously until it reaches to one of the statement/expression that starts with the await operator. At this point the code executes asynchronously until the await statement/expression execution is complete. It's that simple!

▨ **Note**   If the method you defined with async modifier did not contain at least one statement/expression with the await operator, complete method will run synchronously. Note that Visual Studio 2012 will give you a warning related to that to make sure you did not miss adding await!

The following code snippet shows the structure of defining an asynchronous method with an asynchronous operation using async and await.

```
public async Task<int> AsynchronousMethodAsync()
{
    //... code goes here that would run synchronously
    //...

    // use await operator to start the asynchronous execution
    int variablename = await CallAsynchronousOperation();

    //... code executes after the asynchronous operation is over
    //... you can also use the returned variablename value

    // write return statement returning an integer value
}
```

Windows 8 Local Folders and Files Management

Windows 8 introduced the *Windows.Storage* class that manages folders, files, and application settings.

- The *Windows.Storage.StorageFile* class represents a file, provides information about the file and access to its content, and even updates them.

- The *Windows.Storage.ApplicationData* class provides access to the application data storage that can be local, roaming or temporary data storage.

- The *Windows.Storage.Streams* class provides capabilities to read and write from sequential or random streams.

In the next section we will be using some of the methods and interfaces introduced in the above-mentioned classes to perform asynchronous reading and writing from the local storage.

> ▨ **Note** Visit Microsoft MSDN site to get more details on the Windows.Storage class - `http://msdn.microsoft.com/en-us/library/windows/apps/br227346.aspx`.

Implementing Local Storage Helper Class

First, select and right click on the Common folder and select Add Item option to add a new class. In the opened Add New Item window, select Class option, name the class to *LocalStorageHelper.cs,* and click Add button to add a blank *LocalStorageHelper.cs* class under Common folder.

Before we start adding required methods, add the reference to the following additional namespaces to support access to local file storage and to perform read and write operations asynchronously.

```
using Windows.Storage;
using System.IO;
using System.Runtime.Serialization;
using Windows.Storage.Streams;
```

Next, define the following generic list objects within the *LocalStorageHelper* class, which will store data in the memory temporarily before saving it to the *WatchList.xml* file or store data retrieved from *WatchList.xml* file.

```
private static List<object> _data = new List<object>();

public static List<object> Data
{
    get { return _data; }
    set { _data = value; }
}

private const string filename = "WatchList.xml";
```

Next we will implement two static generic asynchronous methods of names *Save* and *Restore* with async public signature. Both methods use the *Windows.System.Threading. ThreadPool.RunAsync* method to create work item with *Normal* WorkItemPriority (a default value) relative to other work items. Here we will call private implementation of *SaveAsync* and *RestoreAsync* to do actual local file save and retrieval. The following code snippet demonstrates these two asynchronous methods. Specially note the use of the await operator!

```
//Save asynchronous method implementation
static async public Task Save<T>()
{
    await Windows.System.Threading.ThreadPool.RunAsync((sender) =>
        SaveAsync<T>().Wait(),
```

```
Windows.System.Threading.WorkItemPriority.Normal);
}

//Restore asynchronous method implementation
static async public Task Restore<T>()
{
    await Windows.System.Threading.ThreadPool.RunAsync((sender) =>
        RestoreAsync<T>().Wait(),
Windows.System.Threading.WorkItemPriority.Normal);
}
```

Now let's implement two private asynchronous *SaveAsync* and *RestoreAsync* methods that would actually implement the logic of saving and retrieving files using *Windows.Storage* class methods and interfaces and using serialization and deserialization.

- In both methods, first we will define a file object of *Windows.Storage.StorageFile* file to create a file of name *WatchList.xml* in the local folder using the *ApplicationData.Current.LocalFolder. CreateFileAsync* method.

- In the *SaveAsync* method, create file as random-access output stream in the ReadWrite mode, and write the stream related to the stock data using serialization (refer the earlier section in this chapter where we decorated the stock class as data contrace).

- For the *RestoreAsync* method, now open the existing file (if it exists) as random-access input stream read, and store the stock data in memory using serialization.

The following code snippet demonstrates the *SaveAsync* asynchronous static private method. Specially note the use of the *await* operator multiple times!

```
static async private Task SaveAsync<T>()
{
    StorageFile sessionFile = await ApplicationData.Current.LocalFolder.
CreateFileAsync
        (filename, CreationCollisionOption.ReplaceExisting);
    IRandomAccessStream sessionRandomAccess =
        await sessionFile.OpenAsync(FileAccessMode.ReadWrite);
    IOutputStream sessionOutputStream = sessionRandomAccess.
GetOutputStreamAt(0);

    var sessionSerializer = new DataContractSerializer
        (typeof(List<object>), new Type[] { typeof(T) });
    sessionSerializer.WriteObject(sessionOutputStream.AsStreamForWrite(),
_data);

    await sessionOutputStream.FlushAsync();
}
```

The following code snippet demonstrates the RestoreAsync asynchronous static private method. Specially note the use of the await operator multiple times!

```
static async private Task RestoreAsync<T>()
{
    StorageFile sessionFile = await ApplicationData.Current.LocalFolder.
CreateFileAsync
        (filename, CreationCollisionOption.OpenIfExists);

    if (sessionFile == null)
    {
        return;
    }

    IInputStream sessionInputStream = await sessionFile.OpenReadAsync();
    var sessionSerializer = new DataContractSerializer
        (typeof(List<object>), new Type[] { typeof(T) });
    _data = (List<object>)sessionSerializer.ReadObject(sessionInputStream.
AsStreamForRead());
}
```

Add SimulatedRandomStocksDetail.csv File

If you want to convert this application in a commercial Windows Store application, you would like to have live updates of the stocks (that are added in the watch list). For that you can potentially use one of stock update services (APIs) provided by the service providers, such as Microsoft Bing, Yahoo, or Google. For the simplicity and focusing on the core subject—implementing MVVM pattern for Windows 8 application—we will not perform integration with such services for the "live update"; however, we will simulate the "live update" scenario by adding a few values of stock details in a comma separated file stored as part of the project and randomly picking values from this file for each added stocks in the watch list.

Create an empty text file with the name *SimulatedRandomStocksDetail.csv* under the *Model* folder. Now you need to add multiple comma separated rows, with each row containing comma separated values for the following fields in the following mention order (first mentioned comes first, and last comes last):

- Stock current price (e.g. 30.30)

- Stock open price (e.g. 30.05)

- Today's change in the stock prices - positive or negative value (e.g. +0.25)

- Range - Today's High and Low Price (e.g. 30.33 - 30.05)

- Range - 52 weeks High and Low Price (e.g. 32.95 - 24.26)

As a sample I have added the following values in the files.

```
15.02,14.99,0.04,14.85 - 15.07,12.45 - 16.79
675,672.87,4.27,671.70 - 677.25,480.60 - 677.25
21.07,21.05,-0.05,20.94 - 21.10,14.02 - 21.19
30.30,30.05,0.25,30.33 - 30.05,32.95 - 24.26
640,636.34,11.77,638.81 - 648.19,354.24 - 648.19
```

In the next chapter we will implement code to retrieve and display these values.

With this maneuver, we have completed the lightweight model classes implementation for our FinanceHub application. As you have noticed, we did all back-end coding in this chapter so there is no visual outcome from this chapter. However, it's a best practice to rebuild the solution (by pressing F6) and make sure you are not getting any errors!

Summary

In MVVM model classes, provide encapsulation of the application data and related business logic, providing maximum data integrity and data consistency. This chapter implemented a lightweight model classes that defined the serializable and deserializable stocks data model and implemented pre-requisites to implement features of Add and Remove stock actions. We also learned some of the new features introduced in .NET Framework 4.5, such as how to implement asynchronous functions and WinRT classes, and methods and interfaces related to the *Windows.Storage* class supporting local data storage and data access features.

The next chapter is the heart of the book and will implement the ViewModel that will tie together Views (implemented in Chapter 2) and Model classes (implemented in this chapter), completing the development of XAML-based FinaceHub Windows 8 application following MVVM pattern.

Do not forget to download the source code. Visit the Chapter 3 folder to look at the source code that we developed in this chapter.

CHAPTER 4

■ ■ ■

Implementing the ViewModel

You have reached to the final step of developing your first Windows 8 XAML application following the MVVM design pattern—implementing the ViewModel of the FinanceHub application!

As part of implementing the ViewModel, this chapter will

- first build the MVVM framework that requires creating a foundation of building separation between the presentation (Views) and the data source (Model).

- then later implement ViewModels of the FinanceHub application that would create a collection of properties and bind them with the built Views.

This implementation will eventually lead us to connect to already implemented data source (the Model) and will enable population of the stocks and stock details information (the View) in our application following the MVVM design pattern. For this we will also make minor changes in the current View definition, where we hardcoded some of the values for the demonstration purpose in Chapter 2.

Building MVVM Framework for FinanceHub Application

With the introduction of XAML and the capabilities of binding data within XAML for Windows 8, WPF, and Silverlight applications, a new design pattern, Model-View-ViewModel (MVVM), emerged. With that, many custom MVVM frameworks, such as MVVM Light (http://mvvmlight.codeplex.com/), Caliburn.Micro (http://caliburnmicro.codeplex.com/), and Cinch (http://cinch.codeplex.com/), are developed, which provide pre-built helper classes, allowing the building of scalable MVVM pattern-bases application rapidly. If you visit these sites, you will notice that these frameworks are getting updated to support Windows 8 WinRT. You should keep an eye on these frameworks, on the progress they make to support the Windows 8 WinRT development. I would recommend exploring the use of one of these frameworks in your LoB WinRT-based Windows 8 application development as these frameworks mature. However, for the purpose of learning the MVVM implementation for Windows 8 application in this book, we are going to implement a minimum footprint of the core services that would require building any MVVM-based Windows 8 application using XAML.

We will implement (or add as a dependency) the following five core services in this section to build the MVVM framework for our application:

- **IoC Container as Dependency** – Inversion of Control (IoC) container is used to implement dependency injection.

- **EventAggregator Class** – is a central container of registered events/messages, which supports pub/sub model, providing decoupling between the publisher and subscriber objects.

- **Navigation Service** – provides abstracted navigation by separating it from the View and enabling it within the ViewModel.

- **ViewModel Locator Class** – is based on the service locator pattern, which enables a clean way of assigning and initializing ViewModel and setting up the DataContext of the control in context, following IoC and dependency injection implementation approach.

- **Delegate Command Class** – allows creation of a typesafe and bindable reusable command (using ICommand interface) in ViewModels.

If you revisit the Setting MVVM Architecture in FinanceHub Project section of Chapter 1, you will notice that we created Dependencies and Infrastructure folders, which we will populate as part of this section to build the required MVVM framework. Let's implement each service one by one in the following sections.

Open the latest FinanceHub project (which you updated last in Chapter 3) to implement ViewModel in this chapter.

IoC Container Dependency

One of the key concepts of building service-oriented and loosely coupled services is to decouple the application components from their dependencies. The Inversion of Control (IoC) is object-oriented design practice, which allows objects coupling at runtime. You would use IoC while implementing dependency injection in order for Views to find the required ViewModels at runtime.

For Microsoft .NET many IoC containers are available for WPF and Silverlight applications and eventually will be available for the WinRT also. In this book we will use a native WinRT IoC container, available on the codeplex site named metroioc (http://metroioc.codeplex.com/), which can be used for Windows 8 WinRT-based applications.

▪ **Note** To get details on available IoC resources and dependency injection containers for .NET, you can visit the blog of Scot Hanselman at http://www.hanselman.com/blog/ListOfNETDependencyInjectionContainersIOC.aspx.

Adding *Metroloc.dll* File to the *Dependencies* Folder

In order to add metroioc container as a dependency to this project, first visit http://metroioc.codeplex.com/ and download the MetroIoc.dll file to your local machine (at any location). Explore that folder, select the MetroIoc.dll file, drag it, and drop it to the Dependencies folder of your FinanceHub project within the Visual Studio solution explorer. You will notice that MetroIoc.dll file is now added to your Dependencies folder.

Adding *Metroloc.dll* File as a Reference to the *Reference* Folder

Now visit the Reference folder, and select Add Reference option to add the MetroIoc.dll as a reference. You will have a Reference Manager window opened—select the Browse option, click on the Browse button, and browse to the project path where you have added the MetroIoc.dll file under Dependencies folder. Select the MetroIoc.dll file displayed in the Reference Manager window, and click OK to add it as a reference under the Reference folder.

■ **Note** It's important that you select the MetroIoc.dll file from the Dependency folder of the project, and not any other location, while adding as a reference. This will add this file as a reference with the relative path and not the absolute path. As a result, it should work with any project structure.

Now you are all set to use MetroIoC container to implement the dependency injection, which will be implemented later in the section during creating ViewModelLocator class.

The EventAggregator Class

As shown in Figure 4-1, an event aggregator service is a central container of registered events/messages which supports pub/sub model to provide decoupling between the publishers (of events/messages as methods) and subscriber (of events/messages for the consumption) objects.

Figure 4-1. An Event Aggregator Service Supporting Pub/Sub Model for Events/Messages

Adding a Blank *EventAggregator.cs* class to the *Infrastructure* Folder

Before we go further in details on how to implement event aggregator class; first select the Infrastructure folder and add a new blank class named EventAggregator.cs.

Now delete the following two references that are not required for this class.

```
using System.Text;
using System.Threading.Task;
```

Next add the following reference that would be required to implement the EventAggregator class.

```
using System.Reflection;
```

Finally, remove the following lines of code that defines the blank EventAggregator class, since we will leverage code from the Caliburn.Micro framework in the next section.

```
class EventAggregator
{
}
```

Leveraging Caliburn.Micro Framework

Microsoft provides an EventAggregator class, which implements an IEventAggregator interface that would be used to get instances of event type. You have an option to use EventAggregator implementation of Prism's; however, its dependency spans across several classes of the Prism framework and thus makes a complex implementation. Instead we are going to leverage EventAggregator implementation from the existing Caliburn.Micro framework available on the codeplex (http://caliburnmicro. codeplex.com/), which follows an Observer pattern to implement the pub-sub model. You need to register a message handler with the aggregator, which will send messages you have subscribed to. It uses WeakReference for publish and subscribe model, hence overcoming issues such as memory leak when using Events.

Visit http://caliburnmicro.codeplex.com/ site and click on the SOURCE CODE tab. You should see a source code tree on the left side, as well a Download link on the top right side menu. Just click on the Download link available to the right side of the page to download complete source code to your local machine.

The next step is to extract the source code and locate the EventAggregator related classes out of the Caliburn.Micro framework and then apply singleton pattern to it to make it simple to use for our application. You can achieve this through the following steps:

1. Extract the downloaded caliburnmicro-40cc11e10a6c.zip file to any location on your machine. You will notice that the source code will be extracted under the caliburnmicro-40cc11e10a6c folder. Note that the file name (and thus folder name) might be different at the time you are downloading it, which will depend on the latest update made on the codeplex site.

2. Open the `Caliburn.Micro.Silverlight` folder located within
    the `src` folder. Note that the WinRT version of updates are made
    under this folder at the time of the writing of this book; this may
    get changed in the future version of Caliburn.Micro framework.
    You should continue visiting the codeplex site to receive the latest
    changes made.

3. Locate two classes, related to the event aggregator, with the
    name `EventAggregator.cs` and `ExtensionMethods.cs` with the
    `Caliburn.Micro.Silverlight` folder.

4. Open the `ExtensionMethods.cs` (either in notepad or in Visual
    Studio) and locate and copy a static extension method `Apply<T>`,
    which is applicable to `IEnumerable<T>`, and paste to the blank
    `EventAggregator.cs` under `FinanceHub.Infrastructure`
    namespace as a static class with the name `ExtensionMethods`.

```
/// <summary>
/// Generic extension methods used by the framework.
    ///Copied from Caliburn.Micro Framework
/// </summary>
public static class ExtensionMethods
{
    /// <summary>
    /// Applies the action to each element in the list.
    /// </summary>
    /// <typeparam name="T">The enumerable item's type.
        /// </typeparam>
    /// <param name="enumerable">The elements to enumerate.
        /// </param>
    /// <param name="action">The action to apply to each item
        /// in the list.</param>
    public static void Apply<T>
        (this IEnumerable<T> enumerable, Action<T> action)
    {
        foreach (var item in enumerable)
        {
            action(item);
        }
    }
}
```

5.   Next open the EventAggregator.cs (either in notepad or in Visual Studio) from the framework, and copy and paste the class to the FinanceHub EventAggregator.cs. Note that we are leveraging the whole class so the complete code is not explained but rather just focused on the modifications we will make to simply the implementation. You can visit the documentation available on the codeplex site to get more understanding on the Caliburn.Micro framework implementation.

6.   The first modification we will make is removing extra code that supports beyond WinRT, which is not a requirement for our purpose. Locating the preprocessor directive #If WinRT, we will leave the code that exists under this directive but remove the #If WinRT directive statement, since we need to support only WinRt option. Next locate the preprocessor directive #else, which is for Silverlight-specific implementation. Select the #else directive and code underneath of that and remove it. Finally, also remove not required #if and #end if directives. Now it's time to apply our custom code, which would implement a singleton pattern for the EventAggregator class and will expose one static property Instance of the type IEventAggregator. We will use this Instance to publish and subscribe events from our viewmodels that we will develop later in this chapter. Add the following code within the EventAggregator class in the beginning of the EventAggregator class implementation:

```
/// <summary>
private static IEventAggregator instance;

/// <summary>
/// Gets the singleton instance.
/// </summary>
public static IEventAggregator Instance
{
    get
    {
        if (instance == null)
            {
                instance = new EventAggregator();
            }
        return instance;
    }
}
```

We finished the implementation of the EventAggregator class; it's time to save your project and compile it to make sure that no compilation error exists.

*The Naviga*tion Service

When following MVVM pattern, we need to implement an abstracted navigation service that will enable navigation to a given page from ViewModel rather than implementing within the View. Since navigation methods are available in View with Frame control, these methods need to be abstracted and be exposed in such a way that navigation can be achieved from ViewModel also. The good news is, if you have experience working with Silverlight Navigation application or Windows Phone 7 application following MVVM pattern, you must have used NavigationService to provide navigation of Views from ViewModel classes. Windows 8 application follows the similar implementation approach with minor changes while implementing the INavigationService interface. Let's get started!

Adding the *INavigationService* Interface

The navigation service is View related as it uses Frame object of Page base class. There are implementations that pass the Frame object to ViewModel, thereby making ViewModel know about the View! However, this violates separation of concern. This also puts restriction of having View and ViewModel classes in the same project, and you cannot develop them as different libraries. To overcome such issues, there are various implementations of NavigationService, following the abstracted INavigationService interface, that define basic navigation methods. This service then injected in ViewModel, thus allowing navigation among views from the ViewModel.

Add a new blank interface named INavigationService.cs under the Infrastructure folder. First, you need to add the following additional references, which would support the navigation events initiated by the Page and Frame classes:

```
using Windows.UI.Xaml.Controls;
using Windows.UI.Xaml.Navigation;
```

In the simplest scenario you would implement the navigation service interface that can support the following navigation features:

- Navigate to a given page

- Visit the previous page using the navigation history

- Be notified when navigation is taking place, as well being allowed to cancel the navigation, if required

Usually you might have implemented the following INavigationService interface for your WPF/Silverlight or Windows Phone applications, which can support the above mentioned navigation features:

```
public interface INavigationService
{
    void InitializeFrame(Frame frame);
    event NavigatingCancelEventHandler Navigating;
```

```
    bool Navigate(Uri pageUri);
    bool Navigate(Uri pageUri, object parameter);
    void GoBack();
}
```

However, when you write a navigation service for Windows 8 application, there is a slight difference in passing parameters for the Navigate method. WinRT does not use uri for the navigation but instead uses an actual Type object, enabling strongly typed navigation. So, for example, you define the Navigate method as shown below (at minimum):

```
bool Navigate(Type type);
bool Navigate(Type type, object parameter);
```

Follow the best practices and structure your project so that it is capable of having XAML pages (views) and view models in different assemblies, extending the above-mentioned definition of the Navigate method by passing type as string.

Add the following code to define the Navigate method for our project:

```
bool Navigate(string type);
bool Navigate(string type, object parameter);
```

Adding the *NavigationService* Class

To implement actual methods defined in the INavigationService interface, select the Infrastructure folder, add a new blank class named NavigationService.cs, and add the following additional references that would support the navigation events initiated by the Page and Frame classes:

```
using Windows.UI.Xaml.Controls;
using Windows.UI.Xaml.Navigation;
```

The following code snippet shows the implementation of this class, which is very self- explanatory. If you quickly review it, you will see that it implements the following:

- Registers a handler for the Navigating event and forwards the event to the listening viewmodels (if any).

- Implements the Navigate method that uses the Frame.Navigate method to load content, which is specified by data type

- Implements the GoBack method, which uses the Frame.GoBack method to navigate to the most recent item in back navigation history

```
namespace FinanceHub.Infrastructure
{
    public class NavigationService : INavigationService
    {
        private Frame _mainFrame;
        public event NavigatingCancelEventHandler Navigating;

        public void InitializeFrame(Frame frame)
        {
            _mainFrame = frame;
        }

        public bool Navigate(string type, object parameter)
        {
            return _mainFrame.Navigate
                (Type.GetType(type), parameter);
        }

        public bool Navigate(string type)
        {
            return _mainFrame.Navigate(Type.GetType(type));
        }

        public void GoBack()
        {
            if (_mainFrame.CanGoBack)
            {
                _mainFrame.GoBack();
            }
        }
    }
}
```

We finished the implementation of the navigation service; it's time to save your project and compile it to make sure that no compilation error exists. Note that this time you may get a warning about the Navigating event is not used, which is obvious since we have not used it yet. So don't worry!

▦ **Note**　Care must be taken when you use the string version of the Navigate method; you must specify the fully qualified name as shown below:

`navigationService.Navigate("FinanceHub.StockDetails");`

Implementing the ViewModelLocator Class

One of the key benefits of implementing a ViewModelLocator class is that not only can you assign and initialize ViewModel and set up DataContext of the control in context by leveraging IoC and dependency injection implementation approach, but you can also provide design time data or design time viewmodel instance for visual studio, or even for expression blend!

To create ViewModel locator class, first select the Infrastructure folder, add a new blank class named ViewModelLocator.cs, and add the following additional references, which would support the implementation of View Model for data binding of different views, using MetroIoc as type container.

```
using FinanceHub.Model;
using FinanceHub.Infrastructure;
using FinanceHub.ViewModel;
using MetroIoc;
```

First of all, we need to create a container and register it with the IoC so it can be used later to register and resolve other types and instances of view models. For this, define a private Lazy class instance of type IContainer. Note that Lazy initialization occurs the first time the Lazy<IContainer>. Value property is accessed. The CreateContainer method initializes this with the native MetroContainer class, provided by MetroIoC. And finally, we are initializing this private instance of container in constructor of the class.

```
private Lazy<IContainer> container;
public IContainer Container
{
    get { return container.Value; }
}

public ViewModelLocator()
{
    container = new Lazy<IContainer>(CreateContainer);
}

private IContainer CreateContainer()
{
    var container = new MetroContainer();

    container.RegisterInstance(container);
    container.RegisterInstance<IContainer>(container);
    container.Register<INavigationService, NavigationService>
        (lifecycle: new SingletonLifecycle());
    return container;
}
```

Note that here we are registering the instance of MetroContainer, using the RegisterInstancce method of MetroIoc. Also we are registering the NavigationService as a singleton, using Register method of MetroIoc and specifying lifecycle as SingletonLifecycle.

We finished the implementation of the ViewModelLocator class; it's time to save your project and compile it to make sure that no compilation error exists. During the implementation of ViewModel classes, we will revisit this class to define the property related to the ViewModel class that will be used for the binding with the respected view.

Implementing the *DelegateCommand* Class

As a XAML developer, you probably are aware and might have implemented delegate command class that would allow you to create a typesafe and bindable reusable command, using ICommand interface, in different ViewModels.

To create delegate command class first select the Infrastructure folder and add a new blank class named DelegateCommand.cs and add the following additional references to support the required implementation.

```
using System.Diagnostics;
using System.Diagnostics.CodeAnalysis;
using System.Windows.Input;
using Windows.UI.Xaml.Input;
```

Now implement a reusable command using ICommand interface, which mainly takes two delegates:

- The first delegate is called when ICommand.Execute(Object param) is invoked.

- The second delegate evaluates the state of the command when ICommand.CanExecute(Object param) is called.

You also have to implement a method, in our case named RaiseCanExecuteChanged(), which triggers the CanExecuteChanged event. This causes the UI element to reevaluate the CanExecute() of the command.

The following code snippet demonstrates the above-mentioned implementation of the DelegateCommand class:

```
public class DelegateCommand : ICommand
{
    private readonly Action<object> _execute;

    private readonly Func<bool> _canExecute;

    /// <summary>
    /// Initializes a new instance of the DelegateCommand class that
    /// can always execute.
    /// </summary>
```

```csharp
/// <param name="execute">The execution logic.</param>
/// <exception cref="ArgumentNullException">
    ///If the execute argument is null.</exception>
public DelegateCommand(Action<object> execute)
    : this(execute, null)
{
}

/// <summary>
/// Initializes a new instance of the DelegateCommand class.
/// </summary>
/// <param name="execute">The execution logic.</param>
/// <param name="canExecute">The execution status logic.</param>
/// <exception cref="ArgumentNullException">
    ///If the execute argument is null.</exception>
public DelegateCommand(Action<object> execute, Func<bool> canExecute)
{
    if (execute == null)
    {
        throw new ArgumentNullException("execute");
    }

    _execute = execute;
    _canExecute = canExecute;
}

/// <summary>
/// Defines the method that determines whether the command can execute
    ///in its current state.
/// </summary>
/// <param name="parameter">
    ///This parameter to be passed as command argument</param>
/// <returns>true if this command can be executed; otherwise, false.
    ///</returns>
[DebuggerStepThrough]
public bool CanExecute(object parameter)
{
    return _canExecute == null ? true : _canExecute();
}

/// <summary>
/// Defines the method to be called when the command is invoked.
/// </summary>
/// <param name="parameter">
    ///This parameter to be passed as command argument</param>
public void Execute(object parameter)
```

```
    {
        if (CanExecute(parameter))
        {
            _execute(parameter);
        }
    }
    /// <summary>
    /// Occurs when changes occur that affect whether
        ///the command should execute.
    /// </summary>
    public event EventHandler CanExecuteChanged;

    /// <summary>
    /// Raises the <see cref="CanExecuteChanged" /> event.
    /// </summary>
    public void RaiseCanExecuteChanged()
    {
        var handler = CanExecuteChanged;
        if (handler != null)
        {
            handler(this, EventArgs.Empty);
        }
    }
}
```

We finished the implementation of the DelegateCommand class; it's time to save your project and compile it to make sure that no compilation error exists.

Implementing ViewModel Classes

So far, we have finished implementation of the MVVM framework that is required as a foundation of building separation between the presentation (Views) and the data source (Model). The next and final step is to implement the following ViewModels under ViewModel folder of the FinanceHub application, which would create a collection of properties and bind them with the built Views.

- **StocksPageViewModel**—is a main ViewModel class that would mainly bind all key stocks related views—StocksPage view, StockInfoView view, and StockDetails view—to display the stocks and related information.

- **StockViewModel**—is a simple ViewModel class that would bind stock to determine the stock is selected or not for RemoveStock view.

- **AddRemoveStockModel**—ViewModel class will bind AddStock and RemoveStock views to enable addition and deletion of stocks.

Let's implement the above ViewModel classes and change the respective Views to bind the Views with the ViewModels.

The StocksPageViewModel ViewModel

The stocks page view model class is a key ViewModel class that would mainly bind all stocks related views—StocksPage view, StockInfoView view, and StockDetails view—to display the stocks and related information.

Adding the *StocksPageViewModel* Class

To create a stocks page view model class, first select the ViewModel folder, add a new blank class named StocksPageViewModel.cs, and add the following additional references to support the required implementation:

```
using System.Windows.Input;
using System.Collections.ObjectModel;
using Windows.UI.Xaml.Controls.Primitives;
using System.Runtime.Serialization;
using FinanceHub.Common;
using FinanceHub.Model;
using FinanceHub.Infrastructure;
```

Derive StocksPageViewModel class from the BindableBase base class, which provides implementation of change notification by implementing the INotifyPropertyChanged interface. The BindableBase class was added automatically by Visual Studio in the Common folder.

```
public class StocksPageViewModel : BindableBase
```

Next define an ObservableCollection of type Stock with backing property as following.

```
private ObservableCollection<Stock> stocks;

public ObservableCollection<Stock> Stocks
{
    get
    {
        return this.stocks;
    }
    internal set
    {
        this.stocks = value;
        this.OnPropertyChanged("Stocks");
    }
}
```

Finally, define the StocksPageViewModel constructor as shown below, which will initialize the stocks collection and navigationservice.

```
private INavigationService navigationService;

public StocksPageViewModel(INavigationService navigationService)
{
    this.Stocks = new ObservableCollection<Stock>();
    this.navigationService = navigationService;
}
```

Updating the *ViewModelLocator* Class

Revisit the Infrastructure folder and open the existing ViewModelLocator class. First add the reference to ViewModel before making additional changes.

```
using FinanceHub.ViewModel;
```

As we define ViewModelLocator in xaml as a resource, the defined property will provide binding to the DataContext property of the respective View/Page. So we need to update the ViewModelSelector class by adding the StocksPageViewModel as a property. Note that IoC will take care of passing required dependency of this class, i.e., NavigationService parameter of the constructor of StocksPageViewModel class. We only need to register the dependency with IoC so that IoC knows about this dependency and can inject them in StocksPageViewModel as a constructor injection. We already registered the INavigationService type with IoC when we created ViewModelLocator class. We will assign Frame property to this NavigationService class from App.xaml.cs later. Note that here we are using RegisterInstance method of MetroIoc to register an instance of Stocks collection as IList<Stock> so that later we will retrieve it from IoC for RemoveStock view using the same registered type. We are using the Resolve method of MetroIoc to resolve navigation service Interface type.

```
public StocksPageViewModel StocksPageViewModel
{
    get
    {
        var VM = Container.Resolve<StocksPageViewModel>();
        Container.RegisterInstance<IList<Stock>>(VM.Stocks);
        return VM;
    }
}

public INavigationService NavigationService
{
    get { return Container.Resolve<INavigationService>(); }
}
```

Note that, here, `Container.Resolve` for `INavigationService` will return the singleton instance of the `NavigationService` class, which was defined in `ViewModelLocator` class earlier, while we implemented basic `ViewModelLocator` class.

Updating *App.xaml* file to add ViewModelLocator as a Keyed Resource

Finally, open the `App.xaml` file of the project to add ViewModelLocator as a keyed resource to make it available at the application level to set up the data context and bind to the required ViewModel classes.

For that, first we have to define xml namespace `infra` as following, to point to `ViewModelLocator` class available in the `Infrastructure` folder of the project:

```
<Application
    x:Class="FinanceHub.App"
    xmlns="http://schemas.microsoft.com/winfx/2006/xaml/presentation"
    xmlns:x="http://schemas.microsoft.com/winfx/2006/xaml"
    xmlns:infra="using:FinanceHub.Infrastructure"
    xmlns:local="using:FinanceHub">
```

Next add a keyed resource `ViewModelLocator` right after the existing AppName keyed resource, as shown below:

```
<infra:ViewModelLocator x:Key="ViewModelLocator"/>
```

Setting Up *DataContext* at Application Level

If you recall, we have `MainPage.xaml`, which serves as a MasterPage of the application. We will set `DataContext` property of it, using `ViewModelLocator`. As a result, all the pages being loaded in `AppFrame` (AppFrame defined as `Frame1` in `MainPage.xaml`, discussed in Chapter 2 during implementing View) will inherit this value and thus can bind to single instance of the `StocksPageViewModel` class.

Visit the `View` folder of the project, open the existing `MainPage.xaml` page, and add the following highlighted DataContext.

```
<Page
    x:Class="FinanceHub.View.MainPage"
    IsTabStop="false"
    DataContext="{Binding StocksPageViewModel,
        Source={StaticResource ViewModelLocator}}"
    xmlns="http://schemas.microsoft.com/winfx/2006/xaml/presentation"
    xmlns:x="http://schemas.microsoft.com/winfx/2006/xaml"
    xmlns:local="using:FinanceHub.View"
    xmlns:d="http://schemas.microsoft.com/expression/blend/2008"
    xmlns:mc="http://schemas.openxmlformats.org/markup-compatibility/2006"
    mc:Ignorable="d" Margin="-1,0,1,0">
```

Remove Default Binding and Resource from *StocksPage.xaml* and *StockDetails.xaml* Views

When we create page of type ItemsPage or SplitPage for Windows 8 application, the template of such pages already provides binding for us to get started with sample data. It's time to remove those default bindings so it can bind to created stocks binding.

Visit the View folder of the project and open the existing StocksPage.xaml page and remove the highlighted default binding DataContext.

```
<common:LayoutAwarePage
    x:Name="pageRoot"
    x:Class="FinanceHub.View.StocksPage"
    DataContext="{Binding DefaultViewModel,
        RelativeSource={RelativeSource Self}}"
    IsTabStop="false"
    ---
    --->
```

Now open the StockDetails.xaml page and remove similar default binding DataContext.

Next revisit StocksPage.xaml page, locate Page.Resources, and change the binding of the resource named itemsViewSource to point to the Stocks collection from Items as following:

```
<Page.Resources>
    <!-- Collection of items displayed by this page -->
    <CollectionViewSource
        x:Name="itemsViewSource"
        Source="{Binding Stocks}"/>
</Page.Resources>
```

Also make the same change to StockDetails.xaml page.

Clean Up Code-Behind of StocksPage View

Let's do some clean-up in the code-behind to remove earlier hard-coded stuff within the views.

Visit the View folder of the project and open the existing StocksPage.xaml.cs code-behind and

- First locate and remove the local Stock class, since we no longer need it.

- Next locate the LoadState method and remove all existing code of the method.

Now open StockDetails.xaml.cs code-behind page, locate the LoadState method, and remove the following line of code:

```
var collection = new ObservableCollection<Stock>();
collection.Add(new Stock
    { Symbol = "MSFT",
        OpenPrice = 30.05M,
        Change = 0.25M,
        CurrentPrice = 30.30M });
this.DefaultViewModel["Items"] = collection;
```

We finished the clean up; it's time to save your project and compile it to make sure that no compilation error exists. At this point, if you run the application, you should see a blank application, as shown in Figure 4-2, with no stock tiles.

Figure 4-2. *Bound FinanceHub Application With No Stock Tiles*

Displaying Stocks using Stocks Collection through ViewModel

At this point, we already bound the views with the Stocks collection, and thus if you add one or more sample stocks in the Stocks collection, you will be able to see it in the view as tiles!

Parsing *SimulatedRandomStocksDetail.csv* file

First let's write code for parsing a sample stock data file—SimulatedRandomStocksDetail.csv file—that we added in the previous chapter under Model folder. This file provides random stock values for user entered symbols. Like any csv file parser, here we will create a new asynchrounous function GetRandomStockData, which will parse the csv file to a collection of type Stock asynchronously, within the existing LocalStorageHelper class residing in the Common folder.

Visit the Common folder and open the LocalStorageHelper class, and first add the following reference so that we can access the Stock class:

```
using FinanceHub.Model;
```

Next add the following code to demonstrate the GetRandomStockData and GetRandomStockDataAsync functions:

```
public async static Task<IEnumerable<Stock>> GetRandomStockData()
{
    return await GetRandomStockDataAsync();
}

static async private Task<IEnumerable<Stock>> GetRandomStockDataAsync()
{
    var stocks = new List<Stock>();
    var data = new List<string[]>();
    var result = await Windows.Storage.PathIO.
        ReadTextAsync("ms-appx:///Model/SimulatedRandomStocksDetail.csv ");
    var stringdata = result.Replace("\r", string.Empty);
    foreach (var line in stringdata.Split('\n'))
    {
        data.Add(line.Split(','));
    }

    foreach (var item in data)
    {
        stocks.Add(new Stock
        {
            CurrentPrice = Decimal.Parse(item[0]),
            OpenPrice = Decimal.Parse(item[1]),
            Change = Double.Parse(item[2]),
            DaysRange = item[3],
            Range52Week = item[4]
        });
    }
        return stocks.AsEnumerable();
    }
}
```

Newly introduced Windows.Storage.PathIO class provides helper methods to read and write a file using an absolute path or URI of the file. As shown above, we have used Windows.Storage.PathIO.ReadTextAsync method to read the SimulatedRandomStocksDetail.csv file and then store each record as a new Stock instance within the stocks collection.

At the time of Visual Studio's building a project, the behavior of the added SimulatedRandomStocksDetail.csv file depends on the value of the BuildAction property of the respective file. When you add SimulatedRandomStocksDetail.csv file, its BuildAction property will set to None, and thus the file will not be compiled in the build process and, as well, will not be included in the project output. We need to include this file as part of the output of the built project but it does not need to be compiled. Select this file and open the Properties window in Visual Studio. You should see the BuildAction property set to None; select the dropdown and change the property value to Content, which will include file to the output of the project but will not be compiled as part of the build process.

Displaying A Default Stock

Now we need to set up code that can call the GetRandomStockData function, map randomly with the available stocks, and bind them with the views by updating existing StocksPageViewModel class. Let's get started!

Visit the ViewModel folder and open the StocksPageViewModel class and add a new asynchronous LoadData method that would call the GetRandomStockData and store the retrieved stocks data into a collection, as well as add MSFT stock and related random information as a default sample stock. Following is the related code:

```
private IEnumerable<Stock> randomStockData;

private async void LoadData()
{
    this.randomStockData = new ObservableCollection<Stock>
        (await LocalStorageHelper.GetRandomStockData());
    this.Stocks.Add(this.GetNewStock("MSFT"));
}
```

If you notice, the LoadData method calls GetNewStock method, which would basically initialize and return the passed stock symbol with random stock data (that is retrieved from the CSV file). The following code shows the GetNewStock method:

```
private Stock GetNewStock(string symbol)
{
    System.Random RndNumber = new System.Random();
    int index = RndNumber.Next(0, 4);
    var newStock = this.randomStockData.ElementAt(index);
    newStock.Symbol = symbol;
    return newStock;
}
```

Notice that we are using System.Random method to randomly select the stock value from the randomStockData collection.

Final step is to call the LoadData method at the initialization to display the stocks. For that you need to call the LoadData method from the constructor of the StocksPageViewModel class (as highlighted below) after initialization of the Stocks collection.

```
public StocksPageViewModel(INavigationService navigationService)
{
    this.Stocks = new ObservableCollection<Stock>();
    this.navigationService = navigationService;
    this.LoadData();
}
```

Take a little pause. We have finished the implementation of the foundation the ViewModel to display the stock information. Save and build the project, and now run the project by pressing F5. You should see now MSFT stock tile in the StocksPage view, as shown in Figure 4-3, which is populated from the random value from the CSV file. Note that you may get different values while you run the project since it randomly selects one of the stock records from the CSV file.

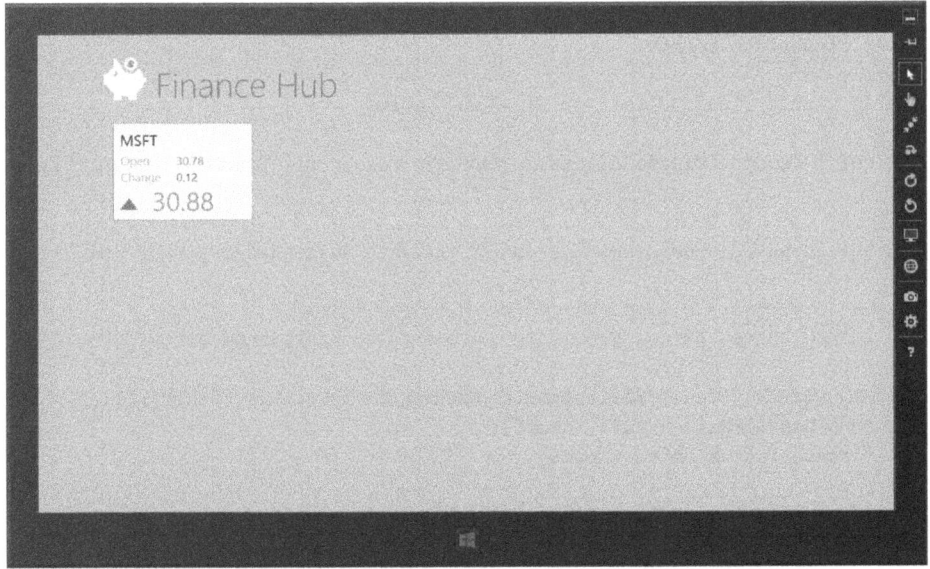

Figure 4-3. *Bound Stock Displayed in the StocksPage view*

Now, if you click on the MSFT stock tile, you should get the StockDetails view displaying MSFT stock detailed information retrieved from the CSV file. Note that you may get different values while you run the project since it randomly selects one of the stock records from the CSV file. Also, remember that at present we have bound only the tiles and not the stock information, which is still hardcoded (as per Chapter 2) and will be changed later in this chapter.

Persisting Stocks State

However, if you visit the Add and Remove stock application bar, you will notice that

- Since we have not implemented the ViewModel related to the Remove stock, the MSFT stock is not displayed in the Remove stock flyout

- You cannot add and persist stocks using Add stock flyout

In this section we will implement required code to persist state of the application to the local storage so next time when you launch the application, it will show you the previously added stock symbols and will assign random values from the CSV file. For this, we will call Save and Restore functions of the LocalStorageHelper class asynchronously that we developed in chapter 3.

First open the App.xaml.cs file, and let's add code to save the Stock collection upon application suspension or termination. For this, we need to add/update the following highlighted code of saving the collection in the existing OnSuspending event defined in App.xaml.cs file. The code serializes the Stock collection to the local storage.

```
using FinanceHub.Model;
using FinanceHub.Infrastructure;
using FinanceHub.Common;

public static ViewModelLocator ViewModelLocator
{
    get { return (ViewModelLocator)Current.Resources["ViewModelLocator"]; }
}

private async void OnSuspending(object sender, SuspendingEventArgs e)
{
    var deferral = e.SuspendingOperation.GetDeferral();
    //TODO: Save application state and stop any background activity

    var stocks = ViewModelLocator.Container.Resolve<IList<Stock>>();
    LocalStorageHelper.Data.Clear();
    foreach (var item in stocks)
    {
        LocalStorageHelper.Data.Add(item);
    }
    await LocalStorageHelper.Save<Stock>();

    deferral.Complete();
}
```

Revisit the LoadData method of the StocksPageViewModel class residing under the ViewModel folder, and update it (the highlighted fonts) so that it can restore the previous state of the application and populate the stocks, if there exists one or more stocks; otherwise, display MSFT stock as a default stock.

```
private async void LoadData()
{
    this.randomStockData = new ObservableCollection<Stock>
        (await LocalStorageHelper.GetRandomStockData());

    await LocalStorageHelper.Restore<Stock>();

    if (LocalStorageHelper.Data.Count > 0)
    {
        foreach (Stock item in LocalStorageHelper.Data)
        {
            this.Stocks.Add(item);
        }
    }
    else
    {
        this.Stocks.Add(this.GetNewStock("MSFT"));
    }
}
```

At present, since we have not implemented the view model for Add and Remove stocks, we will revisit state persistence back again when we develop view model for add/remove stocks.

Compile and run the project to make sure you are not getting any error. You should still get the same output as shown in Figures 4-3 and 4-4.

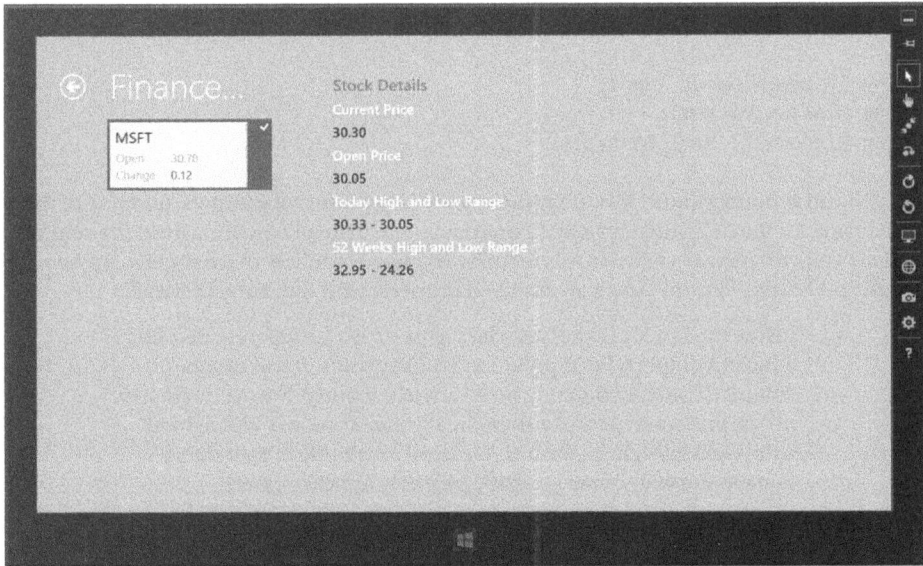

Figure 4-4. *Bound Stock Details Displayed in the StockDetails view*

> ■ **Note**   At this point, for the first time when you compile and run the project, you may get
> an error on the `Restore` method, which we used within the `LoadData` method of the
> `StocksPageViewModel` class. This is potentially a defect with the current WinRT RC
> release. The solution I have found is to first comment out the `await LocalStorageHelper.`
> `Restore<Stock>();` line and run the project. At this time, you should not get any error.
> Now you select the `Suspend` and `Shutdown` option from the Debug Control menu (which
> appears only while you are running the project), which will suspend and then shut down
> the application. Revisit the class and uncomment the `Restore` method, and from this time
> onwards you should not be getting any error.

Wiring Stock Information in Stock Details Page

So far, we bound basic things to show tiles of stocks as a startup page and also to persist
data to local storage. Now we will wire up navigation to the StockDetails page to show
detailed stock information of the selected stock. For that, we need to set binding for
`ItemClick` event of our `GridView` control named `itemGridView`. Since Windows 8 Release
Preview and Blend 5 Release Preview edition do not support the EventToCommand
behavior yet and Blend behaviors and triggers are not available yet to bind to events
other than Command, we will create one attached property helper class that will
overcome this limitation and allow the binding of the `ItemClick` event to our ViewModel
StocksPageViewModel's ICommand implementation.

First create a new `public` class named `ItemClickHelper` in the `Common` folder and the
following additional references to support our need:

```
using System.Windows.Input;
using Windows.UI.Xaml;
using Windows.UI.Xaml.Controls;
```

As you probably know, Visual Studio comes up with sets of snippets, and one of them
is to create for the dependency/attached property. So instead of writing from the scratch,
which is bit complex, we will use this feature. You need to follow these steps to update
`ItemClickHelper` class to create an attached property with the name `Command`:

- Inside the `ItemClickHelper` class, type `propa` (snippet for defining
  attached property) and press the TAB key twice. It will create
  complete code for defining an attached property! Now you will also
  notice that some part of automatically added code is highlighted
  with a yellowish background. We need to provide proper detail
  there to finish defining attached property as per our need.

- First you will notice that the `int` part of the `GetMyProperty`
  method is selected; type `ICommand` and press the TAB key. You will
  notice that appropriate changes are made throughout the code.

- Next it will select the MyProperty part of the GetMyProperty method type Command to create the property name GetCommand. Appropriate changes are made throughout the code.

- Next the selection will shift to ownerclass; type ItemClickHelper and press TAB key.

- Next the selection will shift to 0 within the PropertyMetaData tag. Type null, CommandPropertyChanged.

You will notice that the CommandPropertyChanged method is not defined, so let's do that now. This method is a callback that will be raised every time by dependency property system when the value of the Command property will be changed. We will wire up the ItemClick event handler of the ListViewBase control, which would support GridView control for the normal view and ListViewControl for the snapped view, as shown below.

```
private static void CommandPropertyChanged
    (DependencyObject d, DependencyPropertyChangedEventArgs e)
{
    // Attach click handler
    (d as ListViewBase).ItemClick += ItemClickHelper_ItemClick;
}
```

To implement the ItemClickHelper_ItemClick event handler as shown below, we will execute the bound command with the Command attached property. This will send a trigger to our ICommand implementation in StocksPageViewModel class when ItemClick event occurs.

```
private static void ItemClickHelper_ItemClick
    (object sender, ItemClickEventArgs e)
{
    // Get ItemView
    var itemView = (sender as ListViewBase);

    // Get command
    ICommand command = GetCommand(itemView);

    // Execute command
    command.Execute(e.ClickedItem);
}
```

Next visit and open the StocksPageViewModel class and create a property StockSelectedCommand of type ICommand, as shown below:

```
private ICommand stockSelectedCommand;

public ICommand StockSelectedCommand
{
    get { return stockSelectedCommand; }
}
```

Next we need to define one additional property with the name `CurrentStock` of type `Stock`, as shown below, which we will use to bind to the `SelectedItem` property of the `itemListView` control, available in the `StockDetails` page displaying stocks:

```
private Stock currentStock;

public Stock CurrentStock
{
    get { return currentStock; }

    set
    {
        this.currentStock = value;
        this.OnPropertyChanged("CurrentStock");
    }
}
```

If you recall, our `Navigation` service implementation will need the `string` to navigate to the page providing a fully qualified path. So visit and open the `ViewModelLocator.cs` class under the `Infrastructure` folder and define the `StockDetails` page type as a fully qualified string, as shown below:

```
public const string StockDetailsViewType = "FinanceHub.View.StockDetails";
```

Now revisit the `StocksPageViewModel` class, and initialize the `StockSelectedCommand` in constructor, as following:

```
public StocksPageViewModel(INavigationService navigationService)
{
    this.Stocks = new ObservableCollection<Stock>();
    this.navigationService = navigationService;
    this.stockSelectedCommand = new DelegateCommand(ExecuteStockSelected);
    this.LoadData();
}
```

The implementation of the new `ExecuteStockSelected` method is shown below, wherein you will set the `CurrentStock` to the parameter that is `ClickedItem` of the `GridView` control and then navigate to the `StockDetails` view.

```
private void ExecuteStockSelected(object param)
{
    if (param != null)
    {
        this.CurrentStock = param as Stock;
    }
    navigationService.Navigate(ViewModelLocator.StockDetailsViewType);
}
```

Finally, open the App.xaml.cs file and pass the MainPage's AppFrame to Navigation service's InitializeFrame method in the existing OnLaunched method, as shown below:

```
protected override void OnLaunched(LaunchActivatedEventArgs args)
{
    ---

    ViewModelLocator.NavigationService.InitializeFrame
        ((rootFrame.Content as MainPage).AppFrame);

    // Place the frame in the current Window and ensure that it is active
    Window.Current.Content = rootFrame;
    Window.Current.Activate();
}
```

At this point, rebuild the project and make sure you are not getting any errors.
The only remaining items are binding remaining part of the views.
For that, first, to bind the Command attached property for GridView and ListView to our ItemClickHelper class, open the StocksPage.xaml page, and update this for itemGridView GridView and itemListView ListView controls, as shown below:

```
<GridView
    x:Name="itemGridView"
    common:ItemClickHelper.Command="{Binding StockSelectedCommand}"
    ---
    ItemTemplate="{StaticResource StockTilesTemplate}"/>

<ListView
    x:Name="itemListView"
    common:ItemClickHelper.Command="{Binding StockSelectedCommand}"
    ---
    ItemTemplate="{StaticResource StockTilesTemplate}"/>
```

Now you need to remove the ItemClicked event implementation of the itemGridView and itemListView. For that, locate ItemClick="ClickedStock" within the itemGridView GridView control and itemListView ListView control, and remove them. Then go to the page code-behind and locate the implementation of the ClickedStock event (see the following code) and remove that code also.

```
void ClickedStock(object sender, ItemClickEventArgs e)
{
    this.Frame.Navigate(typeof(StockDetails));
}
```

Next open the `StockDetails.xaml` page and bind the `itemListView` `ListView` control's `SelectedItem` property to `CurrentStock`, as shown below:

```
<ListView
    x:Name="itemListView"
    ...
    SelectionChanged="ItemListView_SelectionChanged"
    SelectedItem="{Binding CurrentStock, Mode=TwoWay}"
    ItemTemplate="{StaticResource StockListTemplate}"/>
```

And add the `DataContext` property of the `StockInfoView` created inside the `itemDetailGrid`, as shown below:

```
<control:StockInfoView Grid.Row="1"
    DataContext="{Binding ElementName=itemListView, Path=SelectedItem}">
</control:StockInfoView>
```

The final step is to open the `StockInfoView.xaml` page and bind each `TextBlock` controls' `Text` property to the related `Stock` property and remove the hardcoded values as shown below:

```
<StackPanel>
    <TextBlock Text="Stock Details"
        Style="{StaticResource HeaderTextStyle}"
        Margin="5" />
    <TextBlock Text="Current Price"
        Style="{StaticResource CaptionTextStyle}"
        Margin="5"/>
    <TextBlock Style="{StaticResource DetailTextStyle}"
        Text="{Binding CurrentPrice}"/>
    <TextBlock Text="Open Price"
        Style="{StaticResource CaptionTextStyle}"
        Margin="5"/>
    <TextBlock Style="{StaticResource DetailTextStyle}"
        Text="{Binding OpenPrice}"/>
    <TextBlock Text="Today High and Low Range"
        Style="{StaticResource CaptionTextStyle}" Margin="5"/>
    <TextBlock Style="{StaticResource DetailTextStyle}"
        Text="{Binding DaysRange}"/>
    <TextBlock Text="52 Weeks High and Low Range"
        Style="{StaticResource CaptionTextStyle}" Margin="5"/>
    <TextBlock Style="{StaticResource DetailTextStyle}"
        Text="{Binding Range52Week}"/>
</StackPanel>
```

We finished the implementation and bound all Views with the data source, using ViewModel. Save and compile and then run the project. You should see the similar screen as Figure 4-3 with the default MSFT stock (this time you may have different values of the stock information, though, based on the generated random number). Now click on the MSFT stock tile; you should be getting the StockDetails page with the MSFT tile and, this time, updated stock detailed information as shown in Figure 4-5. Notice the values displayed about the stock; this time it's different, compared to what we received last from the data source (due to random selection).

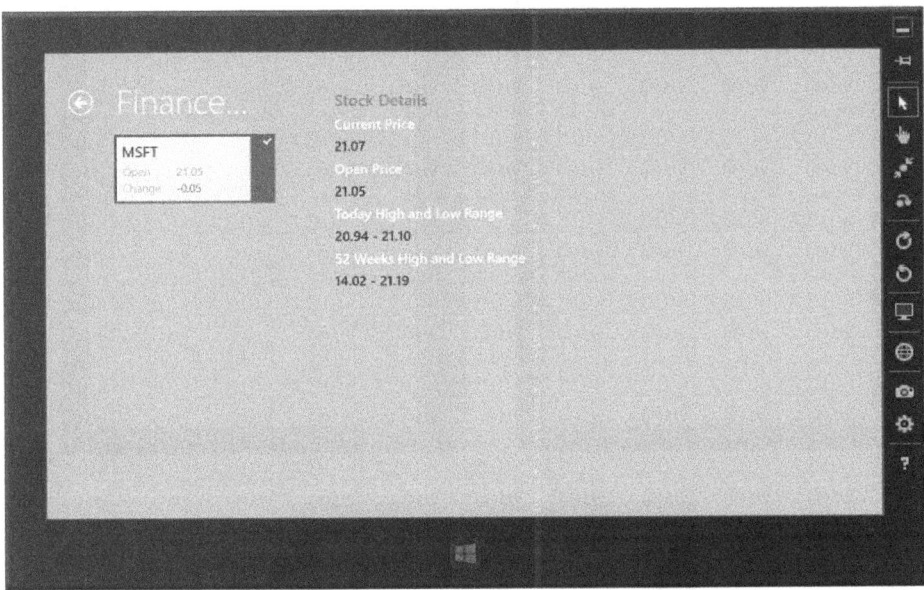

Figure 4-5. *Bound Stock Information Displayed in the StockDetails View*

As you probably know, it's the same operating system, Microsoft Windows 8, which you will use for your regular desktop/laptops as well the tablets (such as Microsoft Surface) and Windows phone. The simulator provides you simulation capabilities to demonstrate your application compatibility with the tablet device, which you will either hold horizontally (as shown in Figure 4-5) or vertically (when you rotate the device to 90 degree). The application would display in the "Normal View" (the views will use GridView in this case) when you are holding the device horizontally and the application would change to the "Snapped View" (the views will use ListView in this case) when you hold vertically by rotating it 90 degree. As you probably noticed, we already took care of this earlier by implementing the proper ItemClickHelper class as well as calling the ItemClick command from both GridView (for Normal view) and ListView (for Snapped view). So let's try now. Compile and rerun the project, and on the simulator you will notice that sixth and seventh commands are to simulate rotating the device 90 degrees clock- or counterclock wise. As shown in Figure 4-6, you will get the StocksPage page, and then when you click on the stock tile, you will get the StockDetails view. First you will see just displays of the StockInfoView, and when you click on the Back button, it will display the stock tile of the StockDetails view. If you click back one time more, you should get back to the main StocksPage view.

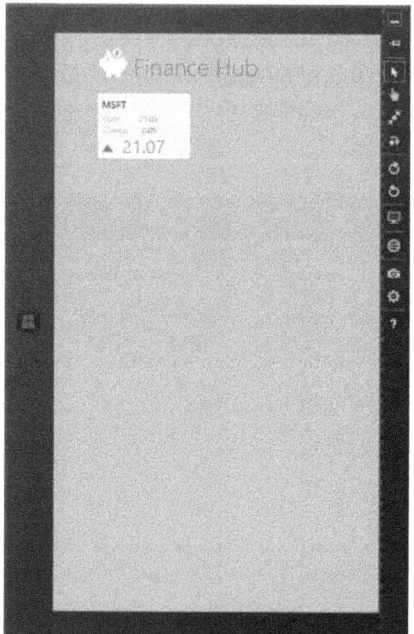
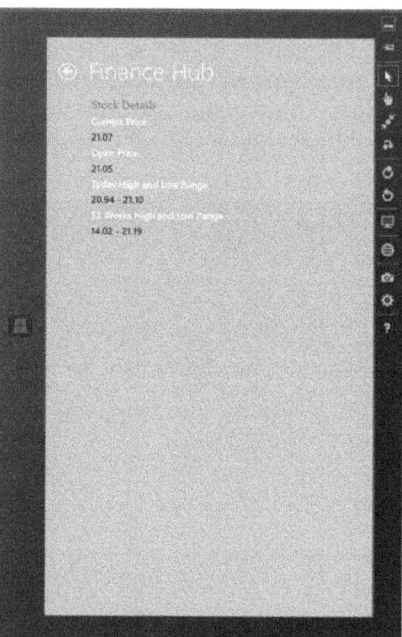
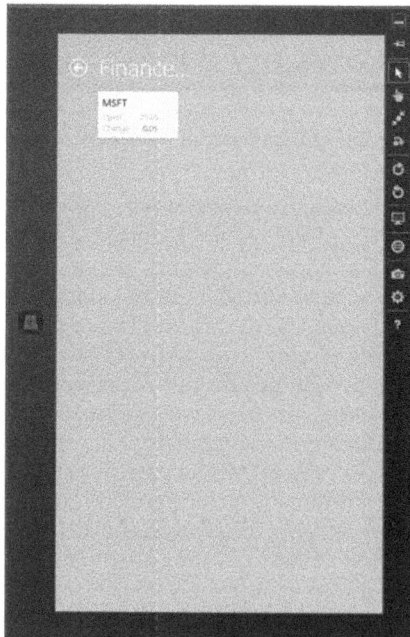

Figure 4-6. *FinanceHub Application Running in the Snapped View*

The AddRemoveStockViewModel ViewModel

So far, we have wired the application navigation that would allow you to navigate application views (StocksPage and StockDetails views), which display bounded stock information in these views. In this section we will create ViewModel, which will allow users to add and remove stocks using the AddStockView and RemoveStockView views. Let's get started!

Adding the *AddRemoveStockViewModel* Class

To create an add remove stock view model class, first select the ViewModel folder and add a new blank public class named AddRemoveStockViewModel.cs. Then add the following additional references to support the required implementation:

```
using System.Windows.Input;
using FinanceHub.Common;
using FinanceHub.Model;
using FinanceHub.Infrastructure;
```

Like StocksPageViewModel class, derive AddRemoveStockViewModel class from the BindableBase base class, which provides implementation of change notification by implementing the INotifyPropertyChanged interface. The BindableBase class was added automatically by Visual Studio in the Common folder.

```
public class AddRemoveStockViewModel : BindableBase
```

Adding New Stock

First we will add logic for adding new stock file in our Stocks collection that we created in the StocksPageViewModel. We will make use of the Event Aggregator to notify StocksPageViewModel about newly added stock symbol.

To capture user input as a stock symbol, we have one textbox in add stock flyout and a button control. Add one property named Symbol of type string to store the user-inputed stock symbol and one ICommand with the name addCommand to bind to the Command property of the button, as shown below:

```
private string symbol;

public string Symbol
{
    get { return symbol; }

    set
    {
        symbol = value;
        this.OnPropertyChanged("Symbol");
    }
}
```

```
private ICommand addCommand;

public ICommand AddCommand
{
    get { return addCommand; }
}
```

Now add AddRemoveStockViewModel constructor and initialize addCommand as following:

```
public AddRemoveStockViewModel()
{
    this.addCommand = new DelegateCommand(ExecuteAdd);
}
```

The implementation of the new ExecuteAdd method is shown below, where you will pass a message (raising event) with ActionEventArgs set to proper action (StockAction. add) and the data (Symbol value) that we want to pass to the receiver component.

```
private void ExecuteAdd(object param)
{
    // Notify Subscribers
    if (this.Symbol != null)
    {
        EventAggregator.Instance.Publish
            (new ActionEventArgs
                { Action = StockAction.Add, Data = this.Symbol });
        this.Symbol = null;
    }
}
```

The receiver component in our case is StocksPageViewMode ViewModel, so visit and open the StocksPageViewModel class and implement an IHandle interface for the ActionEventArgs type as following:

```
public class StocksPageViewModel : BindableBase, IHandle<ActionEventArgs>
```

And now comes the implementation of the IHandle interface, where we will check for duplicate stock symbol before adding it.

```
public void Handle(ActionEventArgs e)
{
    if (e.Action == StockAction.Add)
    {
        if (this.Stocks.Count > 0 && !(this.Stocks.Where
            (c => c.Symbol.ToUpper() ==
                e.Data.ToString().ToUpper()).Count() > 0))
```

```
    {
        this.Stocks.Add(this.GetNewStock(e.Data.ToString().ToUpper()));
    }
  }
}
```

Finally, before we jump to change the XAML pages, we need to subscribe to EventAggregator by adding the following code in the existing constructor of the StocksPageViewModel as shown below.

```
public StocksPageViewModel(INavigationService navigationService)
{
    this.Stocks = new ObservableCollection<Stock>();
    this.navigationService = navigationService;
    this.stockSelectedCommand = new DelegateCommand(ExecuteStockSelected);
    EventAggregator.Instance.Subscribe(this);
    this.LoadData();
}
```

Now let's bind the AddNewStock.xaml view. Open the XAML page, and apply binding to the existing properties

- The Text property of the related textbox control to the Symbol property and

- The Command property of button control to the AddCommand property

The following highlited code demonstrates the above implementation:

```
<TextBox x:Name="txtSymbol" Text="{Binding Symbol, Mode=TwoWay}"
    HorizontalAlignment="Left" TextWrapping="Wrap"
    VerticalAlignment="Top" Margin="5" Width="380"/>
```

```
<Button Content="Add" Command="{Binding AddCommand}"
    HorizontalAlignment="Left"  VerticalAlignment="Top" Margin="5"/>
```

And set the DataContext property of the AddNewStockView view to AddRemoveStockViewModel at UserControl level as shown below:

```
<UserControl
    x:Class="FinanceHub.View.AddStockView"
    DataContext="{Binding AddRemoveStockViewModel,
        Source={StaticResource ViewModelLocator}}"
    xmlns="http://schemas.microsoft.com/winfx/2006/xaml/presentation"
    xmlns:x="http://schemas.microsoft.com/winfx/2006/xaml"
    xmlns:local="using:FinanceHub.View"
    xmlns:d="http://schemas.microsoft.com/expression/blend/2008"
    xmlns:mc="http://schemas.openxmlformats.org/markup-compatibility/2006"
```

```
mc:Ignorable="d" Width="400" Height="130"
d:DesignHeight="300"
d:DesignWidth="400">
```

The final step is to update the ViewModelSelector class by adding the AddRemoveStockViewModel as a property. We are again going to use the Resolve method of MetroIoc to resolve AddRemoveStockViewModel ViewModel type. Open the ViewModelLocator class and add the following code:

```
public AddRemoveStockViewModel AddRemoveStockViewModel
{
    get { return Container.Resolve<AddRemoveStockViewModel>(); }
}
```

It's time to check if the implement code for adding stocks is working or not. Compile and run the project in the debug mode. Bring up the application bar menu, either by right clicking or by swiping your figure from bottom screen side upwards or top screen side downwards, and click on the Add button. You should see the Add Stock flyout and enter the stock symbol (it can be any text since we are not validating against the real time services), and as soon as you click the Add button, the stock should appear on the StocksPage view with the random values assigned from the CSV file. Add a couple of more stocks, and you will probably see the stock tiles look as in Figure 4-7 within StocksPage view.

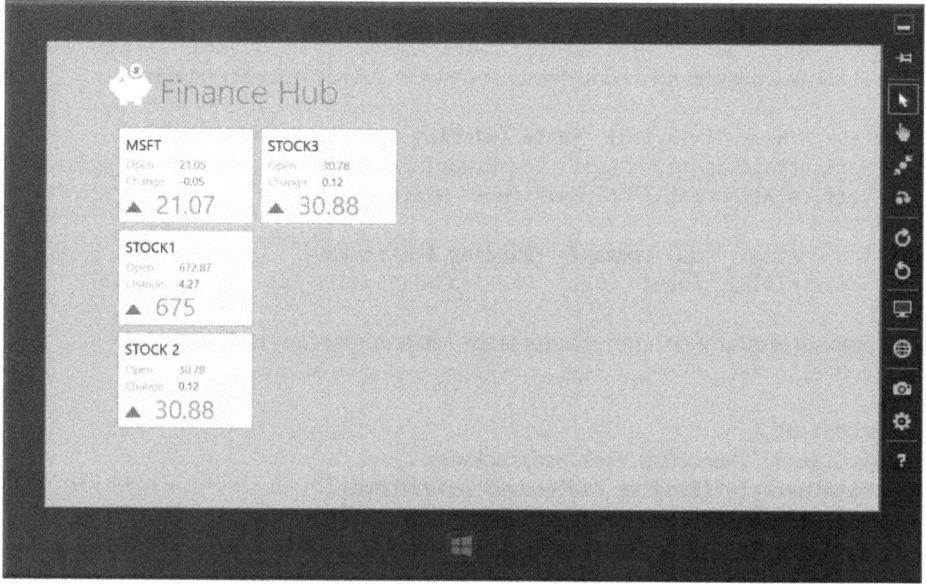

Figure 4-7. StocksPage View with Multiple Stocks Added Using the Add Stock Command

If you click on one of the stocks (in Figure 4-8, it's Stock1), then you should see the StockDetails view, which will display the stock information related to the selected stock, as shown in Figure 4-8.

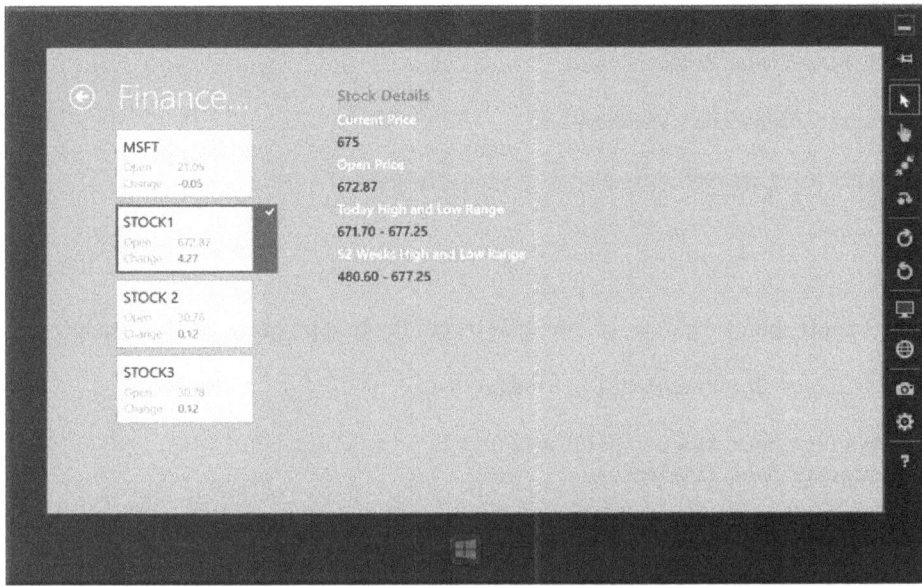

Figure 4-8. *StockDetails View with Multiple Stocks Displaying the Selected Stock Information*

Note that, in the StockDetails view, you can switch from one stock to other stock to get detailed information or even add new stocks through Add stock command. The added stocks will be displayed in the StockDetails view at the end of the stock list, displayed on the left side.

Now it's time to test if the local storage is working or not. Suspend and Shutdown the running project from Visual Studio, and then rerun the FinanceHub application. You should see that all added stocks are restored and are displayed in the same order as they were added in the StocksPage view. The output should be similar to what you see in Figure 4-7 and then Figure 4-8.

Removing Stock

If you have by chance clicked on the Remove button within the application bar, you will notice that the Remove Stock flyout still does not contain any stocks.

To remove one or more stocks, we will be showing a list of current stock symbols with related checkbox, allowing the user to check one or more stock symbols and remove the selected ones from the application. For this, we need to extend the existing Stock class to have additional Boolean type IsSelected property, which will indicate whether to remove stock or not. To add this property, select the ViewModel folder and create a new public StockViewModel class, add required additional references, and then derive this class from the BindableBase, as we did for the earlier ones. The following is the related code:

```
using FinanceHub.Common;
using FinanceHub.Infrastructure;
using FinanceHub.Model;

namespace FinanceHub.ViewModel
{
    public class StockViewModel : BindableBase
    {
    }
}
```

To next update the class, add the IsSelected Boolean property, as shown below:

```
public class StockViewModel : BindableBase
{
    public Stock Stock { get; set; }
    private bool isSelected;

    public bool IsSelected
    {
        get { return isSelected; }
        set
        {
            isSelected = value;
            this.OnPropertyChanged("IsSelected");
        }
    }
}
```

Now reopen the AddRemoveStockViewModel class, and first add the following additional reference:

```
using System.Collections.ObjetModel;
```

Next create a collection of type StockViewModel and ICommand RemoveCommand, as following:

```
private ObservableCollection<StockViewModel> stocks;
public ObservableCollection<StockViewModel> Stocks
{
    get
    {
        return this.stocks;
    }
}
```

```
    internal set
    {
        this.stocks = value;
        this.OnPropertyChanged("Stocks");
    }
}

private ICommand removeStockCommand;
public ICommand RemoveStockCommand
{
    get { return removeStockCommand; }
}
```

Now add a new AddRemoveStockViewModel constructor and initialize removeStockCommand as following:

```
public AddRemoveStockViewModel(IList<Stock> stocks) : this()
{
    this.Stocks = new ObservableCollection<StockViewModel>
        (stocks.Select(c => new StockViewModel { Stock = c }).ToList());
    this.removeStockCommand = new DelegateCommand(ExecuteRemove);
}
```

The implementation of the new ExecuteRemove method is shown below, wherein you will pass a message (raising event) with ActionEventArgs set to proper action (StockAction.Remove) and the data (Stock) that we want to pass to the receiver component for each stock selected to be removed.

```
private void ExecuteRemove(object param)
{
    var stockToRemove = this.Stocks.
        Where(c => c.IsSelected).Select(c => c.Stock);
    if (stockToRemove.Count() > 0)
    {
        foreach (var item in stockToRemove)
        {
            EventAggregator.Instance.Publish
                (new ActionEventArgs
                    { Action = StockAction.Remove, Data = item });
        }
    }
}
```

Now go back to the Handle method of the StocksPageViewModel class, and modify it to add support for remove stock, as shown below (highlighted items):

```
public void Handle(ActionEventArgs e)
{
    if (e.Action == StockAction.Add)
    {
        if (this.Stocks.Count > 0 && !(this.Stocks.Where
            (c => c.Symbol.ToUpper() ==
                e.Data.ToString().ToUpper()).Count() > 0))
        {
            this.Stocks.Add(this.GetNewStock(e.Data.ToString().ToUpper()));
        }
    }
    else
    {
        this.Stocks.Remove(e.Data as Stock);
    }
}
```

The final step is to set up required DataContext and set up binding to the RemoveStockView view. To implement that, select the View folder and open RemoveStockView.xaml file. Now locate ListView and bind to the Stocks collection, and bind SelectedItem property to the Symbol. Bind CheckBox control to Stock.Symbol and bind the Button control's Command property to RemoveStockCommand. The following highlighted code demonstrates that.

```
<ListView
    ItemsSource="{Binding Stocks}"
    SelectedItem="{Binding Symbol, Mode=TwoWay}"
    Background="{StaticResource AppBarBackgroundThemeBrush}">
    <ListView.ItemTemplate>
        <DataTemplate>
            <CheckBox
                Content="{Binding Stock.Symbol}"
                IsChecked="{Binding IsSelected,Mode=TwoWay}" />
        </DataTemplate>
    </ListView.ItemTemplate>
</ListView>

<Button Content="Remove Selected"  HorizontalAlignment="Stretch"
    Command="{Binding RemoveStockCommand}" Grid.Row="1"  ></Button>
```

And finally, set the DataContext property of the RemoveStockView view to AddRemoveStockViewModel at UserControl level, as shown below:

```
<UserControl
    x:Class="FinanceHub.View.RemoveStockView"
    DataContext="{Binding AddRemoveStockViewModel,
```

```
Source={StaticResource ViewModelLocator}}"
xmlns="http://schemas.microsoft.com/winfx/2006/xaml/presentation"
xmlns:x="http://schemas.microsoft.com/winfx/2006/xaml"
xmlns:local="using:FinanceHub.View"
xmlns:d="http://schemas.microsoft.com/expression/blend/2008"
xmlns:mc="http://schemas.openxmlformats.org/markup-compatibility/2006"
mc:Ignorable="d"
Height="300" Width="250"
Background="{StaticResource AppBarBackgroundThemeBrush}"
d:DesignHeight="300"
d:DesignWidth="400">
```

With the above update we have completed the implementation of the ViewModel and, thus, the implementation of the Windows 8 FinanceHub application in XAML following MVVM pattern. Compile and run the project in the debug mode. You should still have the similar features, but now, if you bring up the application bar and click on the Remove button, you should now see the Remove Stock flyout with all the current stock symbols populated with related checkboxs. You can make multiple selections of the stocks that are to be removed. Figure 4-9 demonstrates that the Remove Stock flyout displays four stocks, and I have selected two stocks to be removed.

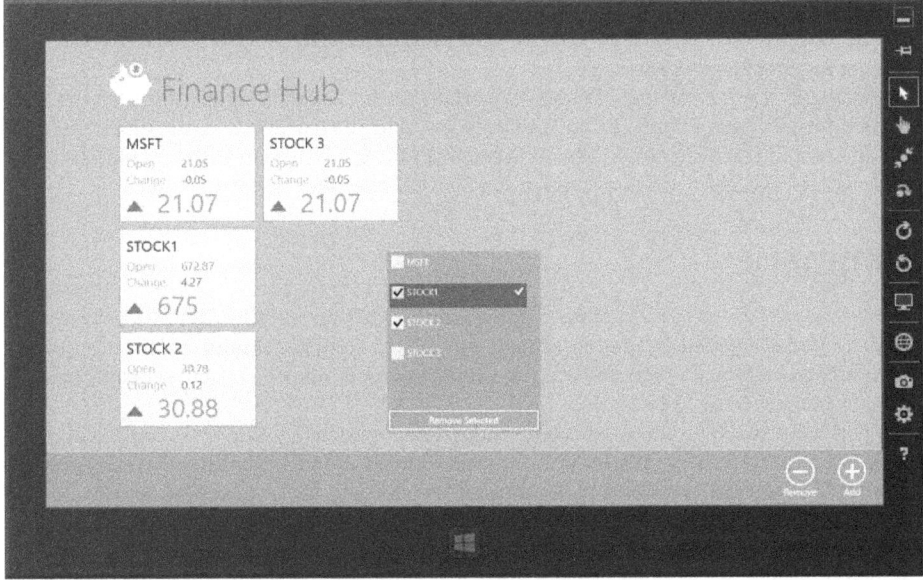

Figure 4-9. *Remove Stock Flyout Enables Multiple Stocks Selection to Remove Selected Stocks*

Now if you click on the Remove Selected button, you will see that the selected stocks should be removed from the StocksPage view, as shown in Figure 4-10.

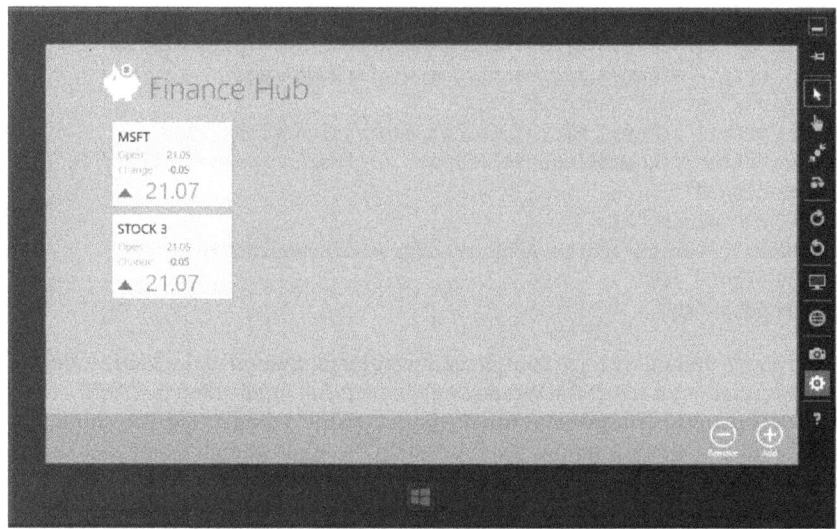

Figure 4-10. *Updated StokcsPage View that does not Include Removed Stocks*

You should see that StockDetails view also reflects the changes you made through adding and removing stocks; you can also perform add and remove stocks actions through the StockDetails view.

Again, let's test if the local storage is working or not. Suspend and Shutdown the running project from Visual Studio, and then rerun the FinanceHub application. You should see that removed stocks are removed from the local storage and only remaining stocks are restored and are displayed in the StocksPage view.

Summary

The ViewModel in the MVVM pattern encapsulates the presentation logic and data for the view. It manages the interactions of views with the required model classes to support data binding and the change notification events by implementing required properties and commands in the ViewModel.

This is the final chapter of implementing MVVM pattern for Windows 8 application using XAML and C#. This chapter mainly implemented the ViewModel, which included the MVVM core framework and then required ViewModel classes to support stocks information binding to StocksPage, StockDetails and RemoveStock views, and application navigation. It also implemented action commands to support stock selection and add and remove stock actions. We also revisited the earlier implementation of the project to remove the hard-coded information and bind it to the ViewModel properties and commands.

In the next chapter we are going to change gears a bit but will still be focused on achieving the same goal. The next two chapters will repeat the development of the same Windows 8 FinanceHub application following MVVM design pattern, but this time using HTML5 and JavaScript.

Do not forget to download the source code. Visit Chapter4 folder to look at the source code that we developed in this chapter.

CHAPTER 5

HTML5, JavaScript, and Windows 8 Applications

If you are a regular .NET developer, then the first four chapters of this book already gave you a solid head start on developing Windows 8 applications using XAML and (probably) your favorite .NET language—C#—following one of the most popular design patterns, the MVVM design pattern. However, if you are a web developer and are more familiar with HTML and JavaScript, then how can you develop Windows 8 applications, also following the MVVM design pattern? As explained during the introduction of the book, the Windows runtime (Win RT) of Windows 8 offers a variety of platforms supporting developers to develop Windows 8 applications. One of the supportable platforms is HTML5 and JavaScript and, of course, supporting MVVM!

The next two chapters will lead you through a rewarding journey of developing the FinanceHub application using HTML 5 and JavaScript, where we will use Windows 8 JavaScript template and will follow the MVVM design pattern.

- This chapter will provide you an overview of the Windows 8 applications development capabilities using HTML5 and JavaScript

- The next and final chapter of this book will implement View, ViewModel, and Model of the FinanceHub application using HTML5 and JavaScript

Before we get into details of how Microsoft Windows Runtime (Win RT), development tools, and third-party JavaScript framework(s) support development of Windows 8 applications (including the support of MVVM design pattern) using HTML5 and JavaScript, let's quickly get a overview of HTML5 and JavaScript.

HTML5 and JavaScript

As Tim O'Reilly defined Web 2.0—*Web 2.0 is the business revolution in the computer industry caused by the move to the Internet as platform, and an attempt to understand the rules for success on that new platform (2006 - http://radar.oreilly.com/2006/12/ web-20-compact-definition-tryi.html)*—today's web applications and services are built on the Internet treating the Internet as a Platform. To support such a revolutionary concept, the existing web development platforms, including one of the most popular and founding platforms—HTML—need some revolutionary changes that can support development of the next-generation web applications, supporting the concept of Web 2.0 and beyond.

The latest version of HTML—HTML5—has gained a wide popularity and is being rapidly adopted across the board to develop and deploy a true cross-platform, cross-browser and cross-device new generation of web applications on the Internet as a platform. With the rise of HTML5 popularity and its integration capabilities with JavaScript development platform, JavaScript is becoming a critical part of the web development platform. As a result, you will start seeing more JavaScript frameworks emerge, along with the integration capabilities of key development platforms and tools, such as integration capabilities with the Microsoft Windows 8 development platform and Microsoft Visual Studio 2012 development tool.

The following are some of the new key features that make HMTL5 such a promising web development platform:

- Set of new semantic and document outlining tags that makes the definition of your web page more meaningful and structured

- New form and input elements to allow managed-input entries with in-built validation

- Introduction of the *canvas* element and JavaScript APIs to support vector graphics and animations

- Introduction of the *audio* and *video* elements supporting native audio and video integration

- Drag and drop API to develop desktop application-like features for the web applications

- Geolocation API to develop location aware applications

- SQL-based database API to enable local storage on client machines supporting offline web applications state

- In-built web worker role to support background processing and the WebSocket interface to implement continuous connection between the HTML5 application and server

- Last but not the least: support to CSS3 to develop rich and interactive web applications

---

▪ **Note** Get *HTML5 Mastery: Semantics, Standards and Styling*, authored by Anselm Bradford and Paul Haines, by visiting Apress site at *http://www.apress.com/9781430238614*. It's also worth reviewing *Beginning CSS3*, by David Powers, available on Apress site at *http://www.apress.com/9781430244738*.

Windows 8 Applications Using HTML5 and JavaScript

If you are a web developer and more familiar with HTML and JavaScript, your preference would be to develop Windows 8 applications using HTML and JavaScript. The Windows runtime (Win RT) of Windows 8 offers a variety of platforms, including using HTML5 and Javascript, supporting the development of Windows 8 applications.

Windows APIs for Windows 8 Store Applications

Microsoft Windows 8 provides two sets of Windows APIs to develop native Windows 8 store applications:

- **Windows Runtime (WinRT)** – is a core language-agnostic platform providing a set of classes, methods, and properties (with *Windows* namespace) to develop applications using C#, VB .NET, JavaScript, C, and C++. For the JavaScript-based Windows 8 applications, the Windows Runtime is available as *Windows* global object.

- **Windows JavaScript Library (WinJS)** – is a set of JavaScript APIs providing advanced JavaScript controls, DOM utilities, CSS styles, support to asynchronous programming, and helper functions (with *WinJS* namespace), which can optionally be used in Windows 8 applications to support more XAML-like abstracted development for Windows 8 applications using HTML5/JavaScript. The WinJS library is available only for JavaScript-based Windows 8 applications, and it's available as *WinJS* global object to the applications.

Windows JavaScript Library

WinJS is a library of objects structured under the *WinJS* namespace enabling object-oriented and advanced programming, including supporting the asynchronous communication, access to the local storage, and capability to define your own classes and namespaces for Windows 8 applications. We will be leveraging some of the key features of the WinJS in the next chapter to implement the FinanceHub Windows 8 application using HTML5/JavaScript, following the MVVM design pattern.

The following provides a high-level overview of namespaces available as part of Windows JavaScript Library:

- **WinJS namespace** – is a root namespace for Windows JavaScript library and also provides the *Promise* object and abstraction to manage asynchronous communication and the *xhr* function that would wrap calls to *XMLHttpRequest* in a promise object.

- **WinJS.Application** – supports application-level features such as storage, application, events management, etc.

- **WinJS.Binding** – provides data and template binding, including capabilities for the declarative binding using *data-win-bind* attribute, which will be useful to develop applications supporting MVVM design pattern.

- **WinJS.Class** – provides helper functions to define classes.

- **WinJS.Namespace** – provides helper functions to define namespaces.

- **WinJS.Navigation** – helps to build basic navigation.

- **WinJS.Resources** – enables resources management to implement globalization and localization features.

- **WinJS.UI** – provides a set of advanced user controls, such as AppBar, Menu, SemanticZoom, ListView, Flyout, etc. Please note that while you add a UI control from the WinJS.UI namespace, you will use the *div* tag in HTML5 and not the direct element name, and you use the *data-win-control* attribute to define the required control. The statement - *<div data-win-control="WinJS.UI.ListView></div>* will add the WinJS ListView control.

- **WinJS.UI.Animation** – supports implementation of Windows animation using custom controls.

- **WinJS.UI.Fragments** – helps to load HTML content programmatically.

- **WinJS.UI.Pages** – supports definition and displaying of *PageControl* objects to implement navigation within your application.

- **WinJS.Utilities** – provides helper functions, such as add and remove CSS classes.

- **Win JS Library Control Attributes** – provides a set of attributes, such as *data-win-control* to specify the type of control and *data-win-bind* attribute to bind a property of an element to a property of data source, to configure Win JS UI controls within HTML markup.

- **Win JS Library Style Sheets** – provides two default styles sheets to provide HTML5/JavaScript based application to Windows 8 theme. Use the *ui-dark.css* stylesheet for defining dark background and light foreground and *ui-light.css* stylesheet for defining light background and dark foreground.

You need to add one of the following stylesheets referent to your HTML markup to provide Windows 8 theme of your choice.

```
<link href="//Microsoft.WinJS.1.0/css/ui-dark.css" rel="stylesheet">
```

Or

```
<link href="//Microsoft.WinJS.1.0/css/ui-light.css" rel="stylesheet">
```

> ■ **Note** Visit Microsoft MSDN site at *http://msdn.microsoft.com/en-us/library/br211377.aspx* to get more information on the Windows API (including Windows JavaScript library) reference for Windows 8 store applications.

Best Practices in JavaScript Development

Believe it or not, JavaScript does follow an object-oriented programming language. It's an interpreted prototype-based programming language. In JavaScript, you define object by creating a constructor function rather than defining a class.

> ■ **Note** Get more details on JavaScript object-oriented programming by visiting *https://developer.mozilla.org/en-US/docs/JavaScript/Introduction_to_Object-Oriented_JavaScript* link.

The following sections of this chapter would describe some of the best practices in JavaScript development that we will be following in our next chapter to develop HTML5/JavaScript-based Windows 8 FinanceHub application following MVVM design pattern.

Global Namespace Pollution and Prevention

If have experience in JavaScript development, then you might have heard about the global namespace pollution in JavaScript. In JavaScript, variables defined outside the function are globally available. These variables are part of the global namespace, and defining them is called global namespace pollution. Thus, if you have defined such variable and you are using any 3rd party JavaScript library that contains any variable with the same name, it will create a conflict with that library. The solution to such problem is using namespace while defining objects and functions. The WinJS really helps here by providing the *define* method of the *Namespace* object as following:

```
WinJS.Namespace.define
    ("ViewModel",
    {
        //other members for the ViewModel object ...
    });
```

In the next chapter you will notice that we will follow a namespace convention while developing model and view model JavaScript functions of our application.

Use of Self

Using *self* is a common JavaScript construct and is required whenever local functions need to refer to the main object. It is not a keyword but is a closure that will reference the current object via a variable named *self.* This is useful to refer to members outside the local function because within the local functions, the variable *this* refers to the inner function itself, not to the outer object. So *self* is being used to maintain a reference to the original *this* even as the context is changing as demonstrated in the following example:

```
WinJS.Namespace.define
    ("ViewModel",
    {
        MyViewModel: WinJS.Class.define(
            function () {
                var self = this;
                self.Title = "";
                ....
                ....
        //Some local function
                this.changeTitle = function () {
                    self.Title = "Hi";
                    ....
```

Using the Strict Mode

The strict mode is a new feature of ECMAScript 5 (the latest standard for JavaScript), which enables you to make JavaScript stricter with enforcement. For example, when the strict mode is enabled, you cannot declare variables without using the *var* keyword.

You can declare strict mode by adding *"use strict"*; at the beginning of the JavaScript file, a program, or a function. The scope of a strict mode depends on its context at file level, program level, or at a function level based on where it is declared. Such declaration is known as a *directive prologue*. Once you will apply the strict mode, if your program does not follow the good programming practice, such as not defining variable using *var* keyword or declaration of the variable outside of the function, it will produce an error.

We will make the use of the strict mode while developing view models and model for the application in the next chapter.

■ **Note** To get more details on the strict mode and related restrictions, visit MSDN site at *http://msdn.microsoft.com/en-us/library/br230269.aspx.*

Module Pattern and Self-Executing Functions

Windows 8 applications written with JavaScript uses a JavaScript design pattern called the module pattern. The module pattern is a common pattern used in JavaScript applications to create private variables, objects, and methods. Anything that you create within the module is encapsulated within the module. Enclosing all of your code within a module prevents the conflicting of it from other libraries. You can create a self-executing module by enclosing the entire content of the file within braces, as shown below (in bold fonts).

```
(
    function () {
    ...

    }
)();
```

In Windows 8 JavaScript application template, the automatically created *default.js* file follows this pattern. The advantage of self-executing function is that it executes automatically when the page that references the JavaScript loads.

Using Constructor Initialization

You should use constructor initialization, or in other words, try to make sure that an object doesn't need any further initialization to be used once it has been constructed.

```
function () {
    "use strict";

    WinJS.Namespace.define("ViewModel", {
        MyViewModel: WinJS.Class.define(
            function () {
                var self = this;
                self.Title = "";
        ...
```

In the above example you can initialize the value of *Title* as following:

```
var vm = new MyViewModel();
vm.Title = "Hi";
```

Instead, following the best practice, you should define *MyViewModel* like following (see bold fonts):

```
function () {
    "use strict";

    WinJS.Namespace.define("ViewModel", {
        MyViewModel: WinJS.Class.define(
            function (title) {
                var self = this;
                self.Title = title;
        . . .
```

And the use it like following:

```
var vm = new MyViewModel("Hi");
```

We will be using this good practice while developing the stock model in the next chapter.

The Knockout JavaScript Framework

There are a few third-party JavaScript frameworks, such as Knockout, Kendo MVVM and Knockback, which provide JavaScript library enabling of easier implementation of HTML5 and JavaScript-based applications following MVVM pattern.

In this book we will specifically leverage the Knockout JavaScript framework, which provides a JavaScript library that simplifies the implementation of dynamic JavaScript UIs by applying MVVM pattern.

- Supports implementation of declarative bindings

- Enables automatic UI-refresh implementation when there is a change in the state of applications data model

- Implements dependency tracking by implicitly setting up chains of relationships between model data, to transform and combine it

- Empowers you to generate template-based user interface, aligned with the model data

We will be leveraging the Knockout JavaScript framework while implementing Add and Remove stocks views in the next chapter.

■ **Note** To get more details and download Knockout JavaScript framework, visit
http://knockoutjs.com/.

Summary

This was an introductory chapter providing you a quick overview of HTML5, JavaScript, and best practices to develop JavaScript program. We also looked at Microsoft Windows 8 development platform and development tools support to develop Windows 8 store applications using HTML5 and JavaScript. Microsoft Windows 8 Runtime not only supports the development of Windows 8 applications using HTML5 and JavaScript in a language-agnostic environment using Microsoft Visual Studio 2012 but also provides a dedicated JavaScript library (WinJS) to develop advanced JavaScript-based Windows 8 store applications.

The next and final chapter of this book will create an HTML5 and JavaScript-based Windows 8 FinanceHub application using one of the Windows 8 JavaScript templates available in Visual Studio 2012 and then implementing View, ViewModel, and Models of the FinanceHub applications, following MVVM design pattern. During this implementation we will also leverage the Knockout JavaScript third-party framework.

CHAPTER 6

View, Model, and ViewModel Structures in HTML5 and JavaScript

I am finishing the final chapter of this book exactly as Windows 8 is released! I am very excited to see that the new operating system from Microsoft is getting delivered, which promises to bring the next generation of touch-optimized Windows store applications.

Without wasting further time, let's implement the FinanceHub Windows 8 application using HTML5 and JavaScript following the MVVM design pattern. In this chapter we will develop this application by covering the following main steps:

- Initial project set up by using a Navigation Windows 8 JavaScript application project template

- Implement the View

- Implement the Model

- Implement the ViewModel

- Implement offline storage using the state persistence

Setting up FinanceHub JavaScript Windows 8 Application Project

Similar to Windows 8 XAML application project templates (for Visual C#, Visual Basic .NET, and Visual C++), Visual Studio 2012 provides a few default Windows 8 application project templates for JavaScript such as Blank App, Grid App, Split App, Fixed Layout App, and Navigation App templates.

Let's create a FinanceHub Windows 8 application using JavaScript Navigation JavaScript Windows 8 application project template. Click on the *New Project* option in Visual Studio 2012; if you have default language selection Visual C#, then you will find

Windows 8 application project templates for JavaScript under the *Other Languages* section of the New Project windows of Visual Studio 2012. Select the *Navigation App* Windows 8 application project template, browse to your desired folder, and name the project to *FinanceHub*. Now click OK to create a new project. You will notice that a new folder *FinanceHub* is created, and the Windows 8 JavaScript Navigation application project is created under your selected folder.

Exploring and Setting up FinanceHub Project

If you open the FinanceHub project and look at the Solution Explorer window, you will find Navigation JavaScript Windows 8 application project structure that is somewhat similar to what you saw during creating FinanceHub application using XAML Windows 8 application project.

The Default Project Structure

The base of the JavaScript navigation template-based project structure is somewhat similar to the base of the blank XAML-based Windows 8 application structure that we went through in Chapter 1. Let's quickly look at key files/folders of the project:

- The *default.html* file available under the root project folder is a main HTML page, which defines the structure of the pagelayout and is a default startup page and will be loaded first while you run the application. Please note that you can change the default start-up page through the *package.appxmanifest* file.

- Under *js* folder, *default.js* file is available, which is a startup, page-related, code-behind JavaScript file that would essentially run at the start of the project and is a key file managing data and user interactions. It also contains *navigator.js* file, which is added by default as part of the Navigation project template and is used to support navigation and provide required container to navigate from one page to other.

- Under *css* folder, *default.css* file is available, which provides a set of default styles that would be applied to the HTML page.

- The *References* folder contains a set of JavaScript and CSS files that get used to develop and run Windows 8 application and provide default themes of the application.

- Under *images* folder, (*Assets* folder for XAML-based Windows 8 application project) a set of 4 PNG icon images are present that are used by the application manifest defining default application logos (large and small application logos to display on the start screen and application logo to be displayed on the Windows Store) and splash screen (to display when the application starts).

- Similar to the XAML-based Windows 8 application project, the *package.appxmanifest* file is an important file that defines the runtime configuration properties, such as name, start page, description, tile-related information, notification, and splash screen, and that enables the capabilities of the Windows 8 application deployment package. Open the *Application UI* tab and set the *Background* color for splash screen to *#9ea7b1*.

- An additional folder *pages* is also added containing default home page of the navigation project. We do not need this since we are going to create our own views. Go ahead and delete the entire folder.

Setting MVVM Architecture in FinanceHub Project

So far, we looked at the default JavaScript Windows 8 application structure. Next we will add some additional folders to support the design and development of the FinanceHub project using MVVM design pattern.

Please add the following four folders as placeholders to support the MVVM design pattern:

- Common – This folder will contain required common JavaScript files.

- Model – This folder will contain JavaScript file to implement the model of the application.

- View – This folder will contain the user interface definition made up of different HTML pages and related JavaScript files and related style sheets.

- ViewModel – This folder will contain JavaScript files implementing the ViewModel of the pages/usercontrols.

Adding Application Logo Files and Splash Screen

To provide custom branding to the FinanceHub application, next define the custom application logos and the splash screen. For that, first replace the default splashscreen and storelogo file with the *splashscreen.png* and *storelogo.png* files provided with the Chapter 6 source code. Then add the additional images (available into the Chapter 6 source code) *AppLogo.png*, *up.png*, and *down.png* by dragging and dropping to the *images* folder of the project.

Implementing the View

As part of implementing a View—the user interface—of the FinanceHub application, we need to add custom HTML pages to define StockPage and StockDetails pages and will update the startup default HTML page to incorporate these newly added pages, as well as defining the add and remove stock flyouts. Let's get started.

Adding StockPages.html Page Control

Select the *View* folder and click on Add New Item to add a new Page Control with the name *StocksPage.html*. You will notice that three files—*StocksPage.html*, *StocksPage.css*, and *StocksPage.js*—are added under the *View* folder. When you add any JavaScript type Page Control a new HTML file along with corresponding CSS and JavaScript file will be added to the project.

Open the *StocksPage.html* file, locate the *header* tag with *aria-label* set to *Header Content*, and update the following highlighted items to add a new application logo and change the page title to *Finance Hub*.

```
<header aria-label="Header content" role="banner">
    <button class="win-backbutton" aria-label="Back" disabled></button>
    <img src="..\\images\AppLogo.png"
        style="height:80px;width:80px;margin-left:110px;margin-top:40px" />
    <h1 class="titlearea win-type-ellipsis" style="margin-left:90px">
        <span class="pagetitle">Finance Hub</span>
    </h1>
</header>
```

Next let's define the key styles required to display the stock items and item text. Open the *StocksPage.css* file and first delete the existing style mentioned below:

```
.StocksPage p {
    margin-left: 120px;
}
```

And now add the following new styles:

```
.StocksPage .itemslist .win-horizontal.win-viewport .win-surface {
    margin-bottom: 60px;
    margin-left: 115px;
    margin-top: 7px;
}

.StocksPage .itemslist {
    height: 100%;
    position: relative;
    width: 100%;
    z-index: 0;
}

.StocksPage .itemslist .win-item {
    background-color:#fff;
    padding:15px;
    height: 130px;
    width: 180px;
}
```

```
.StocksPage .itemtext {
 font-size:15pt;
 float: left;
 color:#808080;
}
```

We are all set to start adding new WinJS user controls to start defining the user interface (View) of the FinanceHub application.

Revisit the *StocksPage.html* file and look for the *section* tag, which is just located below the *header* tag. First delete the existing following content:

```
<p>Content goes here.</p>
```

Now add a new *WinJS.UI.ListView* control, as shown following under the *section* tag:

```
<section aria-label="Main content" role="main">
    <div class="itemslist"
            data-win-control="WinJS.UI.ListView"
            data-win-options="{ selectionMode: 'none'}"></div>
</section>
```

Next let's define an item template for the above-added *WinJS.UI.ListView* control within the *body* tag as shown below, which will be used to display each item in the *ListView* control:

```
<body>
<!-- This template is used to display each item in the ListView declared
below. -->
    <div class="itemtemplate" data-win-control="WinJS.Binding.Template">
        <div >
            <h2 style="color:#4E6485"></h2>
            <div class="itemtext">Open</div>
            <div style="margin-left:85px;font-size:15pt;color:#6a7bba"></div>
            <div class="itemtext" >Change</div>
            <div style="margin-left:85px;font-size:15pt;" >
            <div></div></div>
            <div style="float: left;margin-left:15px;margin-top:15px">
                <img style="height:25px" />
            </div>
            <div style="margin-left:85px;margin-top:10px;font-
size:20pt;color:#759CC8">
            </div>
        </div>
    </div>
    ....
</body>
```

Note that this template is still not completely defined. The big missing portion is binding the template, which we will do at later stage in this chapter, when we will implement the ViewModel of the application.

Next jump to the *StocksPage.js* file, and we will apply the above defined item template to the *ListView* within the *ready* event handler, as shown below:

```
ready: function (element, options) {
    // TODO: Initialize the page here.
    var listView = element.querySelector(".itemslist").winControl;
    listView.itemTemplate = element.querySelector(".itemtemplate");
    listView.element.focus();
},
```

Finally set the *StocksPage.html* as home page by opening the *Default.html* file, and under a *body* tag, update the existing *ContentHost data-win-control* of *Application. PageControlNavigator* to point home page to *StocksPage.html* by setting *data-win-options* as shown below.

```
<body>
    <div id="contenthost"
            data-win-control="Application.PageControlNavigator"
            data-win-options="{home: '/View/StocksPage.html'}"></div>
</body>
```

At this point, if you compile the project and run it in the Simulator mode, you should see a custom FinanceHub splash screen and a main application startup page with FinanceHub application logo and application title but no content. Believe me, it's a good start!

We will revisit this page later in this chapter to finish the data-binding implementation.

Adding StockDetails.html Page Control

Select the *View* folder and click on Add New Item to add a new Page Control with the name *StockDetails.html*, which is available under the JavaScript tab. You will notice that three files—*StockDetails.html, StocksDetails.css*, and *StocksDetails.js*—are added under the *View* folder (when you add any JavaScript type Page Control).

Open the *StockDetails.html* file and locate the *header* tag with *aria-label* set to *Header Content*. Now change the page title to *Finance Hub*.

```
<header aria-label="Header content" role="banner">
    <button class="win-backbutton" aria-label="Back" disabled></button>
    <h1 class="titlearea win-type-ellipsis">
        <span class="pagetitle">Finance Hub</span>
    </h1>
</header>
```

To define the key styles required to display the stock details and header information, open the *StockDetails.css* file and first delete the existing style mentioned below:

```
.StockDetails p {
    margin-left: 120px;
}
```

And next add the following new styles:

```
.StockDetails {
    -ms-grid-columns: 350px 1fr;
    display: -ms-grid;
    height: 100%;
    width: 100%;
}

    .StockDetails .itemlistsection {
        -ms-grid-row: 2;
        margin-left: 106px;
    }

        .StockDetails .itemlistsection .itemlist {
            height: 100%;
            position: relative;
            width: 100%;
            z-index: 0;
        }

    .StockDetails .itemlistsection .itemlist .win-item {
        background-color:#fff;
        -ms-grid-columns: 110px 1fr;
        -ms-grid-rows: 1fr;
        display: -ms-grid;
        height: 90px;
        width: 180px;
        padding:10px;
    }

    .StockDetails .detailsection {
        -ms-grid-column: 2;
        -ms-grid-row-span: 2;
        -ms-grid-row: 1;
        margin-left: 70px;
        margin-top: 120px;
        overflow-y: auto;
```

```
        padding-right: 120px;
        position: relative;
        z-index: 0;
    }

.captionStyle {
        color:#fff;
        font-weight:500;
        font-size:16pt;

}

.detailStyle {

        color:#0026ff;
        font-weight:500;
        font-size:16pt;
        margin-bottom:10px;
}

.headerStyle {
        color:#6a7bba;
        font-weight:600;
}
```

We are all set to start adding new WinJS user controls to start defining the user interface (View) of Stock Details of the FinanceHub application.

Revisit the *StockDetails.html* file and look for the *section* tag, which is just located below the *header* tag. First delete the existing following content:

```
<section aria-label="Main content" role="main">
    <p>Content goes here.</p>
</section>
```

Now add a new *WinJS.UI.ListView* control, as shown below:

```
<div class="itemlistsection">
    <div class="itemlist" id="itemlistView"
            data-win-control="WinJS.UI.ListView"
            data-win-options="{ selectionMode: 'single', tapBehavior:
'toggleSelect'}">
    </div>
</div>
<div class="detailsection" id="stockInfoView" aria-atomic="true"
        aria-live="assertive">
    <h2 class="headerStyle" >Stock Details</h2>
    <div class="captionStyle">Current Price</div>
    <div class="detailStyle" ></div>
```

```
        <div class="captionStyle">Open Price</div>
        <div class="detailStyle" ></div>
        <div class="captionStyle">Today High and Low Range</div>
        <div class="detailStyle" ></div>
        <div class="captionStyle">52 Weeks High and Low Range</div>
        <div class="detailStyle" ></div>
</div>
```

Next define an item template for the above-added *WinJS.UI.ListView* control within the *body* tag as shown below, which will be used to display each item in the *ListView* control:

```
<body>
    <div class="itemtemplate" data-win-control="WinJS.Binding.Template">
        <div>
            <h2 style="color:#4E6485"></h2>
            <div style="font-size:15pt;float: left;
color:#808080">Open</div>
            <div style="margin-left:85px;font-size:15pt;color:#6a7bba" >
</div>
            <div style="font-size:15pt;float: left;
color:#808080">Change</div>
            <div style="margin-left:85px;font-size:15pt;"><div></div></div>
        </div>
    </div>
    ....
</body>
```

Next jump to the *StockDetails.js* file, and we will apply the above-defined item template to the *ListView* within the *ready* event handler, as shown below:

```
(function () {
    "use strict";
    var ui = WinJS.UI;

    WinJS.UI.Pages.define("/View/StockDetails.html", {
        // This function is called whenever a user navigates to this page. It
        // populates the page elements with the app's data.
        ready: function (element, options) {
            // TODO: Initialize the page here.
            var listView = element.querySelector(".itemlist").winControl;
            listView.itemTemplate = element.querySelector(".itemtemplate");
            listView.layout = new ui.ListLayout();
        },
        ....
```

At this point, if you compile the project and run it in the Simulator mode, you should see the same output, a custom FinanceHub splash screen and main application startup page with FinanceHub application logo and application title but no content, as shown in Figure 6-1 below.

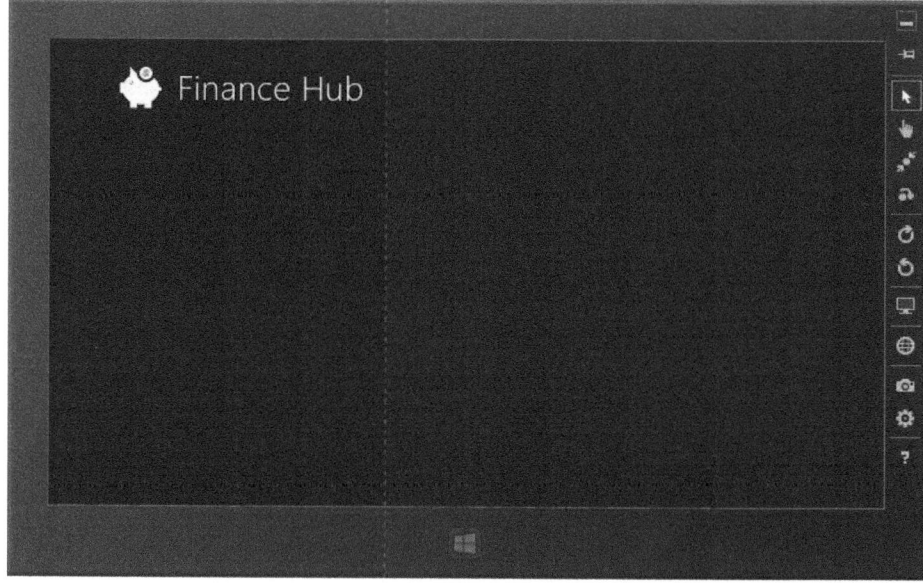

Figure 6-1. *Finance Hub application with partial views implemented*

We will revisit this page later in this chapter to finish the data binding implementation.

Enhancing default.html Page

The *default.html* page will serve as the master page and will contain additional *<div>* markups for hosting Windows 8 app bar for the FinanceHub application containing Add stock and Remove stock buttons. This page will also contain markups for Add and Remove stock flyouts.

Adding AppBar

Open the *default.html* page and add the application bar by adding the *WinJS.UI.AppBar* control with two buttons for add and remove stocks actions just below *contenthost* in the *body* tag.

```
<div id="appbar" data-win-control="WinJS.UI.AppBar" style="background-
color:#9EA7B1">
    <button data-win-control="WinJS.UI.AppBarCommand"
        data-win-options=
            "{id:'cmdAdd',label:'Add',icon:'add',section:'global',tooltip:'
Add',
                type:'flyout', flyout:'addStockFlyout'}">
    </button>
    <button data-win-control="WinJS.UI.AppBarCommand"
        data-win-options=

            "{id:'cmdDelete',label:'Remove',icon:'remove',section:'global',
tooltip:'Delete',
                type:'flyout', flyout:'removeStockFlyout'}" >
    </button>
</div>
```

As you noticed above, we have used *addStockFlyout* and *removeStockFlyout* as *type* value for add and remove stocks buttons. Let's define these flyouts right below the added appbar code.

Adding Add Stock Flyout

For the *addStockFlyout* we will use the *WinJS.UI.Flyout* control and will allow the user to input the new stock information and add it, as shown below, immediately after appbar code:

```
<div id="addStockFlyout" data-win-control="WinJS.UI.Flyout" >
    <div id="addStockFlyoutMessage"></div>
    <input id="addStockText" placeholder="Enter a symbol (e.g., MSFT)" />
    <br /><br />
    <button id="addStockButton" style="color:#fff">Add</button>
    <br /><br />
</div>
```

Adding Remove Stock Flyout

And for the *removeStockFlyout* we will also use the *WinJS.UI.Flyout* control and will allow the user to select one or more stocks from the existing stock list through check box and then remove the selected ones. For that we define a table with input control as checkbox and span tag within the flyout, which is our item template for showing the list of stocks to remove with checkbox. Add the following code to achieve this immediately after the add stock flyout code.

```
<div id="removeStockFlyout" data-win-control="WinJS.UI.Flyout"
    data-win-options="{width:'wide'}" >
        <table>
            <tbody>
                <tr>
                    <td >
                        <input type="checkbox"/>
                        <span></span>
                    </td>
                </tr>
            </tbody>
        </table>
        <button id="Button1" style="color:#fff">Remove Selected</button>
        <br /><br />
</div>
```

Later in this chapter, when we will implement the ViewModel, we will be using the KnockoutJS framework for binding the data to these flyouts.

At this point if you compile the project and run it in the Simulator mode, you should see the same output, a custom FinanceHub splash screen and then main application page with application logo and application with no content. However, this time if you right click or slide from bottom on your touch screen mode, you should see the appbar with add and remove stocks buttons, as shown in Figure 6-2.

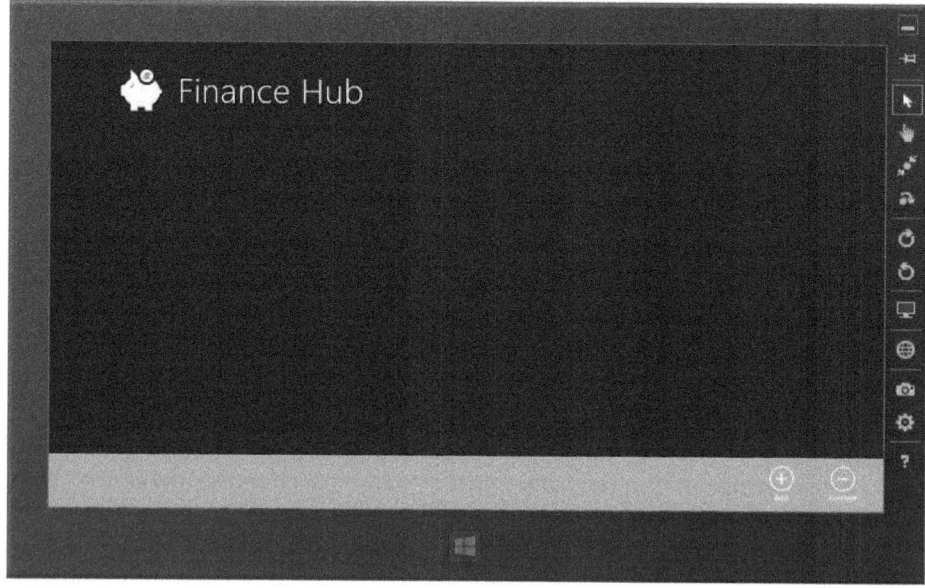

Figure 6-2. *Finance Hub application with partial views implemented*

Click on the Add and Remove buttons and you should see related flyouts displayed (with no content yet, though)!

Implementing Converters

We need to develop two *WinJS.Binding.converter* functions: one for showing the up and down arrow (using the *up.png* and *down.png* images added under the *images* folder) and second for showing current stock value as red or green font, based on value of the change as positive (final outcome would be up arrow and green font) or negative (final outcome would be down arrow and red font).

For this, add a new JavaScript file name *Converters.js* under the *Common* folder and add the following lines of code that define these two converters using *WinJS.Binding. converter* and exposed them in the *FinanceHub.Converters* namespace:

```
(function () {
    "use strict";

    WinJS.Namespace.define("FinanceHub.Converters", {
        ChangeArrowConverter: WinJS.Binding.converter(function (value) {
            return value >= 0 ? "..\\images\\up.png" : "..\\images\\down.png";
        }),

        ChangeColorConverter: WinJS.Binding.converter(function (value) {
            return value >= 0 ? "#108104" : "#C02C01";
        })
    });
})();
```

Create FinanceHub Application Branding

You may decide to apply your unique and custom application that is different from the default Windows library for styles, which you can achieve by overriding the Windows Library for styles. In our case we need to apply background color and page title color of our choice. For that add new Style Sheet named *styles.css* under *css* folder and add the following code:

```
body
{
  background-color:#B3BDE1;
}

.pagetitle
{
  color:#585A8E;
}
```

121

Now open *default.html* and add reference to the newly added style sheet *styles.css* just under the existing *default.css* reference, as following:

```
<link href="/css/styles.css" rel="stylesheet" />
```

Now run the application and you will see that background color and title text foreground color is applied as defined in the custom style sheet, which you can see in Figure 6-3.

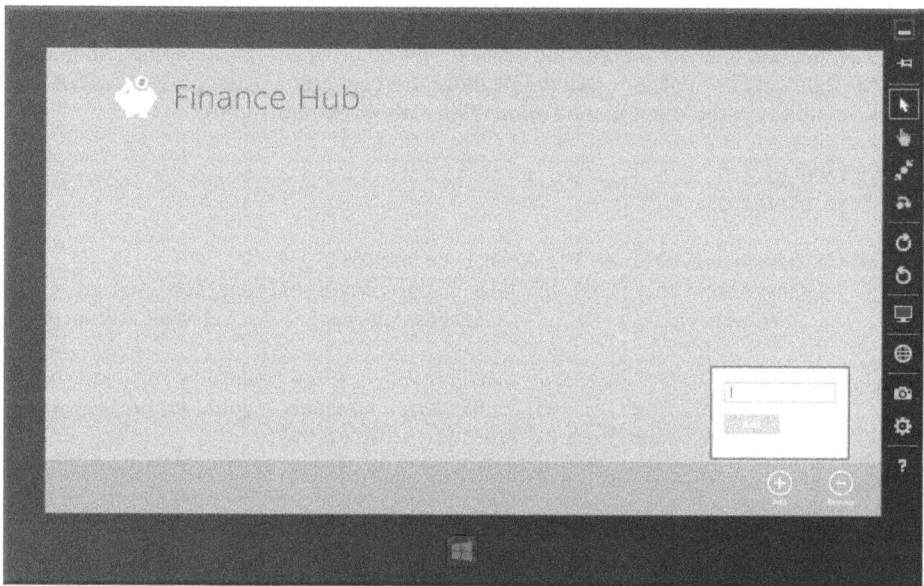

Figure 6-3. *Finance Hub application with custom styles*

Implementing the Model

We successfully implemented the foundation of the View building key user interface of the application in the previous section. Now it's time to implement the model of the application. While we implemented the Model for the XAML-based project in Chapter 3, you noticed that the implementation is pretty straightforward. It includes definition of the stock information (as a class) and also defining a local data source that would help to provide simulated price of the added stocks to your application in random manners.

Define Stock Class

The stocks data model requires a data model that at minimum implements a class supporting the properties to support the following six information pieces about the stock:

- Stock symbol (e.g. MSFT)

- Stock current price (e.g. 30.30)

- Stock open price (e.g. 30.05)

- Today's change in the stock prices - positive or negative value (e.g. +0.25)

- Range - Today's High and Low Price (e.g. 30.33 - 30.05)

- Range - 52 weeks High and Low Price (e.g. 32.95 - 24.26)

To incorporate the above mentioned information, create the Stock class object containing the properties—Symbol, PercentChange, OpenPrice, ClosePrice, Change, and DaysRange.

In JavaScript world, we will define single model class *Stock* following the JavaScript Module pattern. Hence the class definition format would typically look like as shown below:

```
(function () {
    "use strict";

    WinJS.Namespace.define("NameSpaceGoesHere", {
        ClassName: WinJS.Class.define(
            function () {
            var self = this;
            //members initialization
            }
            //private members, methods and properties
    )}
    )
})();
```

To follow that, first go and select the Model folder and add a new JavaScript file with the name *Stock.js*. Open the blank *Stock.js* file and add the following code to define a stock class with the above mentioned properties:

```
(function () {
    "use strict";

    WinJS.Namespace.define("FinanceHub.Model", {
        Stock: WinJS.Class.define(
            function (symbol, currentPrice, openPrice, change, daysRange,
range52Week) {
```

```
            this.Symbol = symbol;
            this.OpenPrice = openPrice;
            this.CurrentPrice = currentPrice;
            this.Change = change;
            this.DaysRange = daysRange;
            this.Range52Week = range52Week;
        }
        , {

            Symbol: undefined,
            OpenPrice: undefined,
            CurrentPrice: undefined,
            Change: undefined,
            DaysRange: undefined,
            Range52Week: undefined
        }),
    });
})();
```

Note that here we have defined *Stock* model class in *FinanceHub.Model* namespace.

Add SimulatedRandomStocksDetail.csv File

If you want to convert this application in a commercial Windows Store application, you would like to have live updates of the stocks (that are added in the watch list). For that you can potentially use one of stock update services (APIs) provided by the service providers, such as Microsoft Bing, Yahoo, or Google. For the simplicity and focusing on the core subject—implementing MVVM pattern for Windows 8 application—we will not perform integration with such services for the "live update." However, we will simulate the "live update" scenario by adding a few values of stock details in a comma-separated file stored as part of the project and randomly picking values from this file for each added stock in the watch list.

As we did in Chapter 3, create an empty text file with the name *SimulatedRandomStocksDetail.csv* under the *Model* folder. Now you need to add multiple comma-separated rows, with each row containing comma-separated values for the following fields in the following mention order (first mentioned comes first, and last comes last):

- Stock current price (e.g. 30.30)

- Stock open price (e.g. 30.05)

- Today's change in the stock prices - positive or negative value (e.g. +0.25)

- Range - Today's High and Low Price (e.g. 30.33 - 30.05)

- Range - 52 weeks High and Low Price (e.g. 32.95 - 24.26)

As a sample, I have added the following values in the files:

```
15.02,14.99,0.04,14.85 - 15.07,12.45 - 16.79
675,672.87,4.27,671.70 - 677.25,480.60 - 677.25
21.07,21.05,-0.05,20.94 - 21.10,14.02 - 21.19
30.30,30.05,0.25,30.33 - 30.05,32.95 - 24.26
640,636.34,11.77,638.81 - 648.19,354.24 - 648.19
```

With this we have completed the lightweight model classes' implementation for our FinanceHub application. As you have noticed, we did all back-end coding in this section, so there is no visual outcome compared to what we implemented as part of the View implementation. However, it's a best practice to rebuild the solution (by pressing F6) and make sure you are not getting any errors!

Implementing the ViewModel

So far we have successfully implemented the foundation of the View by building key user interface of the application and the Model by implementing data model and simulated data source definition in the previous sections. Now it's time to implement the ViewModel of the application.

As part of the ViewModel implementation, we will implement key ViewModel classes that would support binding of stocks-related information to the defined views as well as supporting add and remove stock actions (using KnockoutJS framework). During this implementation we will revisit the existing Views and update them to apply data biding.

In addition, we will also develop helper classes to implement local storage supporting CRUD operations on the stored stocks in the CSV format.

Define StocksPageViewModel Class and Bind to the Views

The *StocksPageViewModel* class is a key class and would mainly bind all stocks-related views—StocksPage view and StockDetails view—to display the stocks and related information.

Adding StocksPageViewModel Class

Select the *ViewModel* folder and add a new JavaScript file with the name *StocksPageViewModel.js*. To start, first open the blank *StocksPageViewModel.js* file and add the following code that will define a bindable List named *Stocks*. Later on, we will populate it with the objects of the *Stock* model that we already defined earlier in Model folder:

```
(function () {
    "use strict";

    WinJS.Namespace.define("FinanceHub.ViewModel", {
        StocksPageViewModel: WinJS.Class.define(
```

```
            function () {
                var self = this;
                self.stocks = new WinJS.Binding.List();
                self.stocks.push(new FinanceHub.Model.Stock
                    ("MSFT", 25, 24, 2, "24.59 - 25.92", "23.22 - 25.76"));

                //Expose the data source
                WinJS.Namespace.define("FinanceHub.Data", {
                    Stocks: self.stocks
                });
            }
            , {
                stocks: undefined,
            }),
    });
})();
```

As you see, the *WinJS.Binding.List* of stocks is defined and is exposed in namespace *FinanceHub.Data* so that you can bind with *StocksPage.html*'s *ListView* control. Note that I have also added a sample stock MSFT so that we can see a single tile once we are done binding to the view.

Now we need to bind the earlier defined *StocksPage* and *StockDetails* views so that we can see the sample MSFT stock.

For that, first you need to open all their HTML files, *default.html, StocksPage.html,* and *StockDetails.html,* and add the following added JavaScript files references under the *head* tag.

```
<!--Reference to model and view model js files -->
<script src="/Common/Converters.js"></script>
<script src="/Model/Stock.js"></script>
<script src="/ViewModel/StocksPageViewModel.js"></script>
```

Please note that here the above order of adding JavaScript file as a reference is important because *StocksPageViewModel.js* is referring the *Stock* class defined in *Stock.js,* so it should be referenced before you reference to the ViewModel.

Binding StocksPage View

Open the *StocksPage.html* from the *View* folder and apply binding for the existing *itemtemplate,* as highlighted in bold below:

```
<div class="itemtemplate" data-win-control="WinJS.Binding.Template">
    <div >
        <h2 data-win-bind="textContent:Symbol" style="color:#4E6485"></h2>
        <div class="itemtext">Open</div>
        <div style="margin-left:85px;font-size:15pt;color:#6a7bba"
            data-win-bind="innerText:OpenPrice"></div>
```

```
<div class="itemtext" >Change</div>
<div style="margin-left:85px;font-size:15pt;"
        data-win-bind=
            "style.color:Change FinanceHub.Converters.
ChangeColorConverter">
    <div data-win-bind="innerText:Change"></div></div>
    <div style="float: left;margin-left:15px;margin-top:15px">
    <img data-win-bind="src:Change FinanceHub.Converters.
ChangeArrowConverter"
            style="height:25px" /></div>
    <div style="margin-left:85px;margin-top:10px;font-
size:20pt;color:#759CC8"
            data-win-bind="innerText:CurrentPrice"></div>
    </div>
</div>
```

You will notice that we are using *data-win-bind* attribute/property of the WinJS control to bind the element with the defined data source in the ViewModel. Note that we have also used two previously developed converter functions in binding elements.

Next look for the *section* tag and apply binding for the *itemDataSource* property of the *WinJS.UI.ListView* control, as following (in bold):

```
<div class="itemslist"
        data-win-control="WinJS.UI.ListView"
        data-win-options=
            "{ selectionMode: 'none', itemDataSource: FinanceHub.Data.
Stocks.dataSource}">
</div>
```

Updating default.js File

Next open the *default.js* file available under the *js* folder, and in the *activated* event handler, look for the following comment text:

```
// TODO: This application has been newly launched. Initialize
// your application here.
```

Add the following lines of code:

```
var vm = new FinanceHub.ViewModel.StocksPageViewModel();
var pageVM = WinJS.Binding.as(vm);
WinJS.Binding.processAll(document.body, pageVM);
```

In the above code, the first line initializes the new instance of the *StocksPageViewModel* class. The second line creates an observable object named *pageVM* from the existing JavaScript object *vm*. This new object also has all the properties of the original object *vm*. In addition to that, the properties of the observable *pageVM* object triggers notification when the properties are changed. In the third line the *WinJS.Binding.processAll()* method is called to perform the actual binding. The first parameter passed to the *processAll()* method represents the root element for the binding. So binding will happen on this element and its child elements. If a *null* value is provided, then the binding happens on the entire body of the *document*, i.e., *document.body*. The second parameter represents the data context. This is the object that has the properties, which are displayed with the *data-win-bind* attributes.

Now run the application, and you should get a default MSFT stock on the home page with the related stock information, as shown in Figure 6-4, but no navigation to the StockDetails view when you click on that.

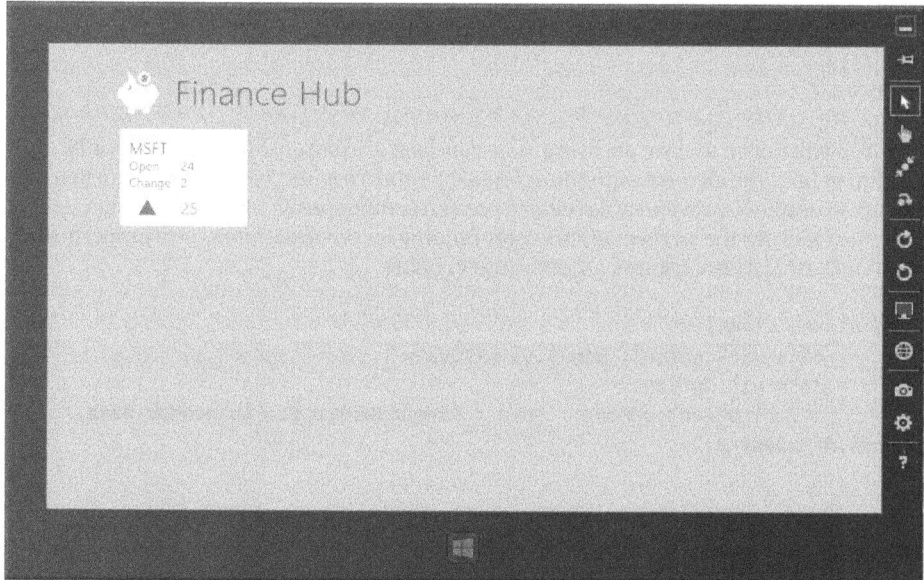

Figure 6-4. *Binding Stock Information to the StocksPage View*

Wiring Up Navigation – StocksPage View to StockDetails View

Now wire up navigation to the *StockDetails.html* page from the *StocksPage.html*, when you click/select one of the stocks from the home page. For this, open the *StocksPageViewModel.js* from the ViewModel, and add following highlighted code:

```
(function () {
    "use strict";

    WinJS.Namespace.define("FinanceHub.ViewModel", {
        StocksPageViewModel: WinJS.Class.define(
```

```
function () {
    var self = this;
    self.stocks = new WinJS.Binding.List();
    self.stocks.push(new FinanceHub.Model.Stock
        ("MSFT", 25, 24, 2, "24.59 - 25.92", "23.22 - 25.76"));
    WinJS.Utilities.markSupportedForProcessing(this.
stockClicked);

WinJS.Utilities.markSupportedForProcessing(this.stockSelectionChanged);

    //Expose the data source
    WinJS.Namespace.define("FinanceHub.Data", {
        Stocks: self.stocks

    });

    //Expose the events and methods
    WinJS.Namespace.define("FinanceHub.Command", {
        StockClicked: self.stockClicked,
        StockSelectionChanged: self.stockSelectionChanged,
    });
}
, {
    stocks: undefined,
    stockClicked: function (e) {

WinJS.Navigation.navigate("/View/StockDetails.html").then(function () {

            FinanceHub.Command.StockSelectionChanged(e);

        });
    },

    stockSelectionChanged: function (e) {
        var ele = document.getElementById('stockInfoView');
        WinJS.Binding.processAll(ele,
            FinanceHub.Data.Stocks.getAt(e.detail.itemIndex));
    },
    }),
    });
})();
```

Here, we have used the *WinJS.Navigation.navigate* method to navigate to the *StockDetails.html* page. We used the promise object and called the *StockSelectionChanged* function residing in the *FinanceHub.Command* namespace. The *StockSelectionChanged* function is set to the currently clicked stock (*e.detail.itemIndex*) as data context of the *stockInfoView* element in *StockDetails* page. So whenever user clicks any stock on StocksPage, the *stockClicked* event will fire, it will navigate to the stock details page, and *stockSelectionChanged* event will set the clicked stock information. The important piece of this code is *WinJS.Utilities.markSupportedForProcessing*, which actually marks a function as being compatible with declarative processing. Declarative processing is performed by *WinJS.Binding.processAll*.

Next you need to bind the *StockClicked* event to the *StocksPage.html* file. For that, open the *StocksPage.html* page, locate the *section* tag, and modify the *data-win-options* attribute for *WinJS.UI.ListView,* as following (highlighted text), to add binding for *oniteminvoked* event.

```
<section aria-label="Main content" role="main">
    <div class="itemslist"
            data-win-control="WinJS.UI.ListView"
            data-win-options="{ selectionMode: 'none',
                                        itemDataSource:
FinanceHub.Data.Stocks.dataSource,

oniteminvoked:FinanceHub.Command.StockClicked}">
    </div>
</section>
```

Binding StockDetails View

At this point, the clicking to the MSFT stock from the StocksPage should work but still no details will display on the StockDetails page. To bind the StockDetails view, we need to apply binding in the *StockDetails.html* page. Open the *StockDetails.html* page and follow the below steps:

Modify the *itemtemplate,* as highlighted below, to add binding:

```
<div class="itemtemplate" data-win-control="WinJS.Binding.Template">
    <div>
        <h2 data-win-bind="textContent:Symbol" style="color:#4E6485"></h2>
        <div style="font-size:15pt;float: left; color:#808080">Open</div>
        <div style="margin-left:85px;font-size:15pt;color:#6a7bba"
            data-win-bind="innerText:OpenPrice"></div>
        <div style="font-size:15pt;float: left; color:#808080">Change</div>
        <div style="margin-left:85px;font-size:15pt;"
            data-win-bind=
                "style.color:Change
FinanceHub.Converters.ChangeColorConverter">
            <div data-win-bind="innerText:Change"></div>
        </div>
    </div>
</div>
```

Modify the binding for the *WinJS.UI.ListView* control *itemlistview,* as following:

```
<div class="itemlistsection">
    <div class="itemlist" id="itemlistView"
            data-win-control="WinJS.UI.ListView"
            data-win-options="{ selectionMode: 'single', tapBehavior:
'toggleSelect',
                itemDataSource: FinanceHub.Data.Stocks.dataSource,
                oniteminvoked:FinanceHub.Command.StockSelectionChanged}">
    </div>
</div>
```

Modify the *detailsection div* tag, as highlighted below, to add the stock information binding:

```
<div class="detailsection" id="stockInfoView" aria-atomic="true" aria-
live="assertive">
    <h2 class="headerStyle" >Stock Details</h2>
    <div class="captionStyle">Current Price</div>
    <div class="detailStyle" data-win-bind="innerText:CurrentPrice" ></div>
    <div class="captionStyle">Open Price</div>
    <div class="detailStyle" data-win-bind="innerText:OpenPrice" ></div>
    <div class="captionStyle">Today High and Low Range</div>
    <div class="detailStyle" data-win-bind="innerText:DaysRange"></div>
    <div class="captionStyle">52 Weeks High and Low Range</div>
    <div class="detailStyle" data-win-bind="innerText:Range52Week"></div>
</div>
```

Now run the application, and you should get a default MSFT stock on the home page with the related stock information. This time, if you click/select the stock, you will get to the StockDetails page with the MSFT (selected) stock information, as shown Figure 6-5.

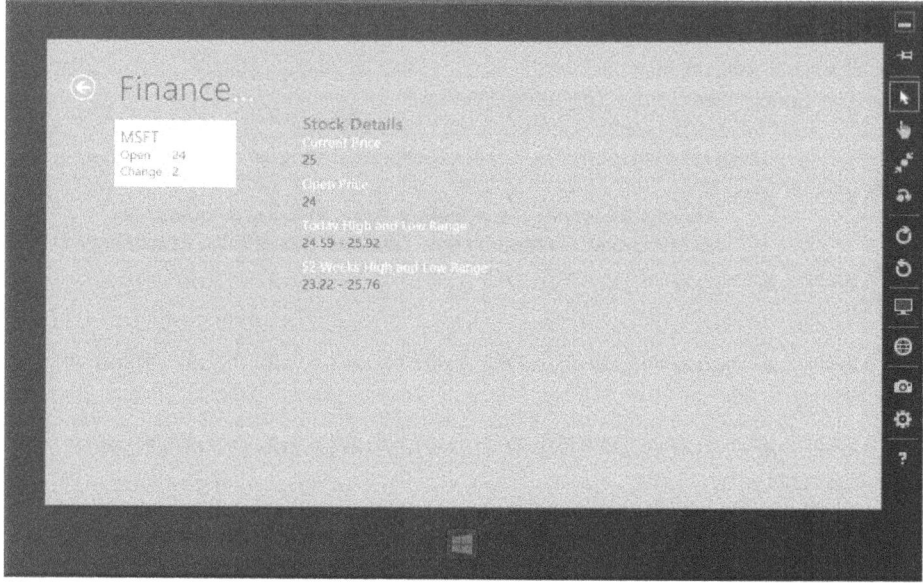

Figure 6-5. *Binding Stock Information with the StocksDetails View*

Implementing Local Storage Helper Class

So far we have made pretty good progress. The application is functioning as desired, but with only the default MSFT stock. Now let's implement the foundation of the feature so that you can add additional stocks and can retrieve the stock values from the simulated sample CSV file containing random stock information.

This section will implement a local storage helper class within the *Common* folder, which would allow us to read and parse the CSV—*SimulatedRandomStocksDetail.csv*—available under the *Model* folder.

To create this class, select the *Common* folder, add a JavaScript file as a new item with the name *LocalStorageHelper.js*, and add the following code, creating the class under *FinanceHub.LocalStorageHelper* namespace.

```
(function () {
    "use strict";

    WinJS.Namespace.define("FinanceHub.LocalStorageHelper", {

        ParseCSV: function (data) {
            var allTextLines = data.split(/\r\n|\n/);
            var rows = [];

            for (var i = 0; i < allTextLines.length; i++) {
                var data = allTextLines[i].split(',');
                var temp = [];
```

```
            for (var j = 0; j < data.length; j++) {
                temp.push(data[j]);
            }
            rows.push(temp);
        }
        return rows;
    },
  });
})();
```

Here we have created a function *ParseCSV, which* will accept the string as an argument and then will split the data and return a resultant array of string.

Next add an additional *GetRandomStockData* function right below the *ParseCSV* function that would read the *SimulatedRandomStocksDetail.csv* file available under the *Model* folder and call the *ParseCSV* function to parse each record of the file. The following is the related code:

```
GetRandomStockData: function () {
    var url = "/Model/SimulatedRandomStocksDetail.csv";
        return WinJS.xhr({ url: url }).then(function (response) {
        return FinanceHub.LocalStorageHelper.ParseCSV(response.responseText);
    });
},
```

Here we have used *WinJS.xhr* function to get the file. This function wraps call to *XMLHttpRequest* in a promise object. This function can be used to call web service, uploading and downloading files.

■ **Note** You can get more information on the *WinJS.xhr* function by visiting Microsoft MSDN site at `http://msdn.microsoft.com/en-us/library/windows/apps/br229787.aspx`.

The final step is to add a reference to this JavaScript file to your project. For that, open the *default.html* file and use the *script* tag to add a reference to the *LocalStorageHelper.js* file, available under the *Common* folder, under the *Reference to model and view model js files* section.

```
<script src="/Common/LocalStorageHelper.js"></script>
```

Define AddandRemoveStockViewModel Class and Bind to the Views

After adding a local storage helper class, now build a ViewModel for the Add and Remove flyouts, which would enable us to add and remove stocks. As mentioned in Chapter 5, we will be using the KnockoutJS framework to implement this ViewModel. Let's get started.

Setting up Project to Use KnockoutJS Library

Get the latest KnockoutJS library by visiting a documentation section of the KnockoutJS website at http://knockoutjs.com/documentation/installation.html and download the latest JavaScript library file to your local folder. At the time of the writing of this chapter, the latest library version is 2.0.0, and the file name is *knockout-2.0.0.js*.

Now visit the *js* folder of the *FinanceHub* project, and add the downloaded KnockoutJS JavaScript library file by using the Add Existing Item option and browsing to the local folder where you have downloaded the file.

The final step is to add a reference to this JavaScript file to your project. For that, open the *default.html* file and use the *script* tag to add a reference to the *knockout-2.0.0.js* file, available under the *js* folder, under the *Reference to model and view model js files* section.

```
<script src="/js/knockout-2.0.0.js"></script>
```

Adding AddRemoveStockViewModel Class

Select the *ViewModel* folder and add a new JavaScript file with the name *AddRemoveStockViewModel.js*. Next we will be adding two functions to this class, which would help us to add stocks and remove stocks; That is where we will be using the KnockoutJS JavaScript library.

Now open the *default.html* file and use the *script* tag to add a reference to the *AddRemoveStockViewModel.js* file, available under the *ViewModel* folder, under the *Reference to model and view model js files* section.

```
<script src="/ViewModel/AddRemoveStockViewModel.js"></script>
```

Adding Add Stock Function to the ViewModel

Open the blank *AddRemoveStockViewModel.js* file and add the following code that defines add stock functionality:

```
(function () {
    "use strict";

    WinJS.Namespace.define("FinanceHub.ViewModel", {
        AddRemoveStockViewModel: WinJS.Class.define(
            function () {

                var self = this;
                self.symbol = ko.observable();
                self.randomStockData = [];

                //Function for Adding new stock
                self.addStock = function () {
                    if (self.symbol() != undefined) {
```

```
                        //check for duplicate
                        for (var i = 0; i < FinanceHub.Data.Stocks.length;
i++) {
                             if (FinanceHub.Data.Stocks.getAt(i).Symbol.
toUpperCase() ==
                                 self.symbol().toUpperCase())
                                 return;
                        }

                        FinanceHub.Data.Stocks.push
                           (self.getNewStock(self.symbol().toUpperCase()));
                        self.stocksVM.push(new StockViewModel(self.symbol().
toUpperCase()));
                        self.symbol("");
                    }
                }

                self.getNewStock = function (symbol) {
                    var num = Math.floor((Math.random() * 3) + 1);
                    var newStock = self.randomStockData[num];
                    newStock.Symbol = symbol;
                    return newStock;
                }

                //Parse SimulatedRandomStocksDetail.csv for sample data
                FinanceHub.LocalStorageHelper.
                    GetRandomStockData().then(function (csvData) {
                    csvData.forEach(showIteration);

                    function showIteration(value, index, array) {
                        self.randomStockData.push(new FinanceHub.Model.Stock
                            ("", value[0], value[1], value[2], value[3],
value[4]));
                    }
                });
            })
        })
    })();
```

The above code basically defines *addStock* function. The function first checks for the duplicate and then assigns stock attributes values randomly, which are retrieved and parsed from the *SimulatedRandomStocksDetail.csv* file, where we use the *GetRandomStockData* function defined in the *LocalStorageHelper* class.

The most important part in the above code is the use of *self.symbol = ko.observable();* statement. It defines the *knockoutJS* observable object. Observables are the special JavaScript objects that can notify subscribers about changes and can automatically update UI; in our case, as soon as you add the stock, it will be updated in the view automatically.

Next select and open the *default.html* file, locate the *addStockFlyout div,* and apply binding as highlighted following:

```
<div id="addStockFlyout" data-win-control="WinJS.UI.Flyout" >
        <div id="addStockFlyoutMessage"></div>
        <input id="addStockText" data-bind="value: symbol"
                    placeholder="Enter a symbol (e.g., MSFT)" />
        <br /><br />
        <button id="addStockButton"
                        data-bind="click:addStock"
style="color:#fff">Add</button>
        <br /><br />
</div>
```

Notice that similarly to WinJS's data-win-bind, KnockoutJS library also uses the *data-bind* attribute to define the binding. Here we bound the *value* and button *click* property of the respective control to the properties *symbol* and *addStock* that we created in the ViewModel earlier.

The final step is to instantiate the ViewModel in *default.js.* For this, open the *default.js* file available under the *js* folder, locate the *activated* event handler, and modify the code, as highlighted below:

```
WinJS.Binding.processAll(document.body, pageVM).then(function () {
    // Activates knockout.js
    ko.applyBindings(new FinanceHub.ViewModel.AddRemoveStockViewModel());
});
```

Here the *ko.applyBindings* method activates knockoutJS and process bindings.

If you run the application at this point, then you should get a default MSFT stock on the home page with the related stock information. Right click or swipe your figure at the bottom of the screen to get the Windows app bar. Click on the Plus Sign (Add) button and add stocks of your choice, using the Add Stock flyout.

You will notice that as soon as you enter a stock symbol and click on the add button, the stock will be added and the values will be assigned from the CSV file and will be displayed on the StocksPage view. Figure 6-6 shows the same, with two stocks added to the home page.

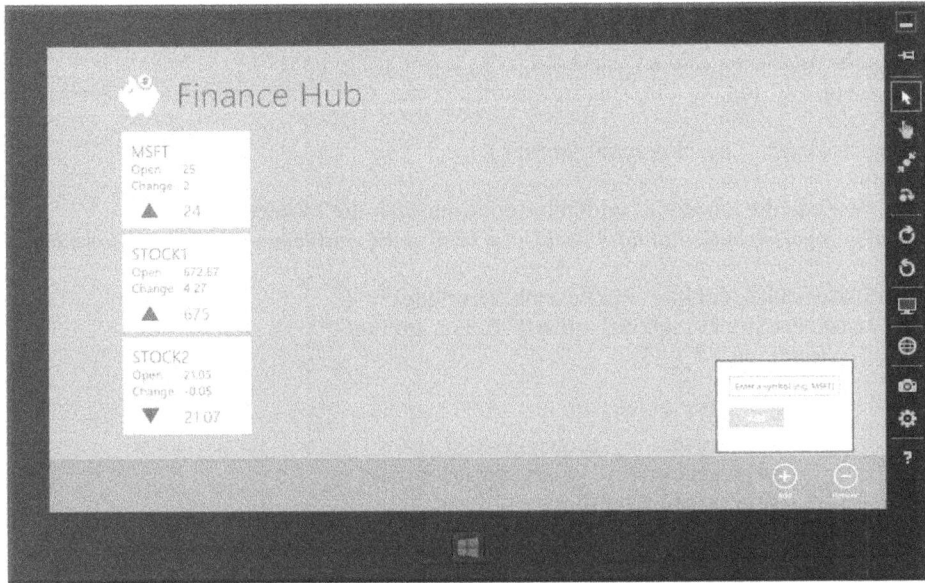

Figure 6-6. *Demonstrating Add Stock Functionality*

Figure 6-7 shows StockDetails view with the added stocks and displays the Stock1 information.

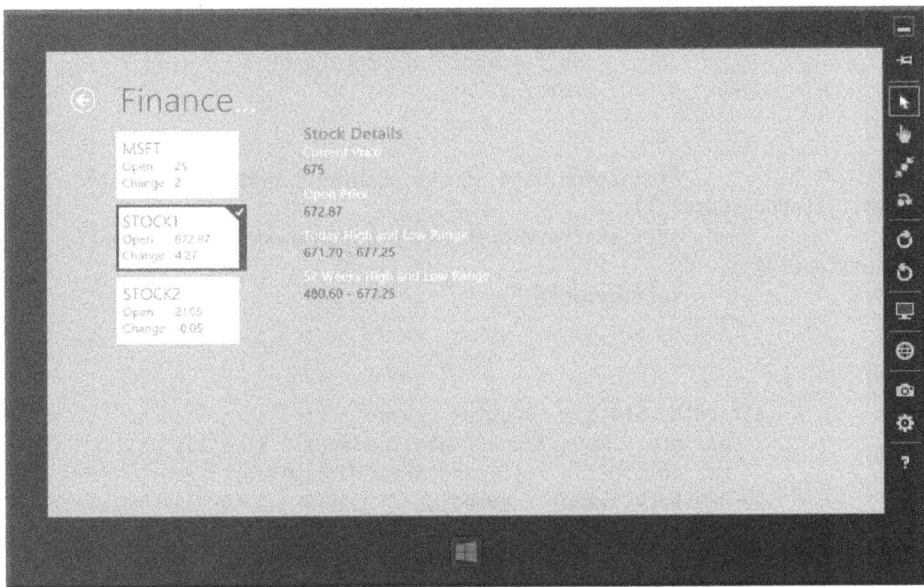

Figure 6-7. *StockDetails View With Additional Added Stocks*

Adding Remove Stock Function to the ViewModel

Open the *AddRemoveStockViewModel.js* file, locate *self.symbol = ko.observable();* statement, and add the following statement just after that to define an *observableArray*.

```
self.stocksVM = ko.observableArray();
```

Now add the following highlighted code just after the *FinanceHub. LocalStorageHelper.GetRandomStockData()* call in the *AddRemoveStockViewModel* file.

```
WinJS.Namespace.define("FinanceHub.ViewModel", {
    AddRemoveStockViewModel: WinJS.Class.define(
        function () {

            var self = this;
            self.symbol = ko.observable();
            self.stocksVM = ko.observableArray();
            self.randomStockData = [];

            //Function for Adding new stock
            self.addStock = function () {
                if (self.symbol() != undefined) {

                    //check for duplicate
                    for (var i = 0; i < FinanceHub.Data.Stocks.length; i++)
{
                        if (FinanceHub.Data.Stocks.getAt(i).Symbol.
toUpperCase() ==
                            self.symbol().toUpperCase())
                            return;
                    }

                    FinanceHub.Data.Stocks.push(self.getNewStock(self.
symbol().toUpperCase()));
                    self.stocksVM.push(new StockViewModel(self.symbol().
toUpperCase()));
                    self.symbol("");
                }
            }

            self.getNewStock = function (symbol) {
                var num = Math.floor((Math.random() * 3) + 1);
                var newStock = self.randomStockData[num];
                newStock.Symbol = symbol;
                return newStock;
            }
```

```
//Parse SimulatedRandomStocksDetail.csv for sample data
FinanceHub.LocalStorageHelper.GetRandomStockData().then(function
(csvData) {
        csvData.forEach(showIteration);

        function showIteration(value, index, array) {
            self.randomStockData.push(new FinanceHub.Model.Stock
                ("", value[0], value[1], value[2], value[3],
value[4]));
        }
    });

    FinanceHub.Data.Stocks.forEach(showIteration);
    function showIteration(value, index, array) {

        self.stocksVM.push(new StockViewModel(value.Symbol));

    }

    //Function for removing the stock
    self.removeStock = function () {

        for (var i = this.stocksVM().length - 1; i >= 0; i--) {
            if (self.stocksVM()[i].isSelected() == true) {
                FinanceHub.Data.Stocks.splice(i, 1);
                self.stocksVM.remove(self.stocksVM()[i]);
            };

document.getElementById("removeStockFlyout").winControl.hide();
        }
    };

    function StockViewModel(data) {

        this.stock = ko.observable(data);
        this.isSelected = ko.observable(false);
    };
  })
})
```

Here, the *forEach* loop on *FinanceHub.Data.Stocks* is to populate the *stocksVM*
array that is a type of *StockViewModel*. The *StockViewModel* is having *isSelected* property,
which will tell us about the stock symbols selected by the user in Remove stock flyout.

The *removeStock* method removes the selected stocks from *FinanceHub.Data.Stocks*
as well as *self.stocksVM*. Note that we are removing stock based on the retrieved index of
the item and using the *splice* method. This is because, as of now, there is no method such
as *removeAt* in *WinJS.Binding.List* available that enables removing item by an index.

Next select and open the *default.html* file, locate the remove*StockFlyout div*, and apply binding as highlighted following:

```
<div id="removeStockFlyout" data-win-control="WinJS.UI.Flyout"
        data-win-options="{width:'wide'}" >
        <table>
            <tbody data-bind="foreach: stocksVM">
                <tr>
                    <td >
                        <input type="checkbox" data-
bind="checked:isSelected"/>
                            <span data-bind="text: stock"></span>
                    </td>
                </tr>
            </tbody>
        </table>
        <button id="Button1" data-bind="click:removeStock"
style="color:#fff">
                    Remove Selected</button>
        <br /><br />
</div>
```

Here we bound the required control properties and button *click* property to populate the existing stocks and enable remove stock functionality.

If you run the application at this point, then you should get a default MSFT stock (notice that the stocks you have entered are not saved yet!) on the home page with the related stock information. Right click or swipe your figure at the bottom of the screen to get the Windows app bar. Click on the Plus Sign (Add) button and add couple of stocks of your choice, using the Add Stock flyout.

Next, click on the Minus Sign (Remove) button on the app bar. This time you should see a list of stocks that exists as part of your application; you can select one or more by clicking the checkbox and then click Remove button to delete them. Figure 6-8 demonstrates the same.

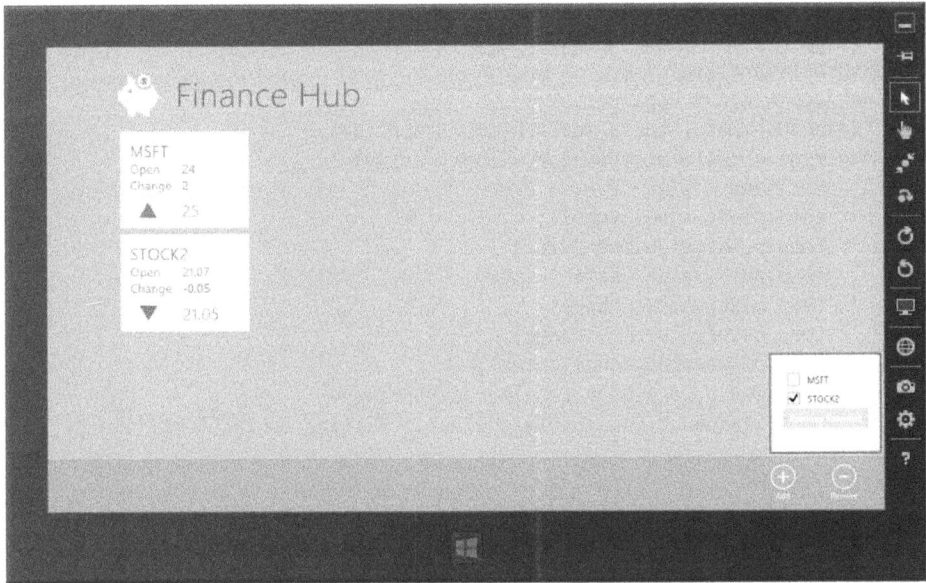

Figure 6-8. *Demonstrating Remove Stock Functionality*

Please note that Add and Remove stocks functionality will be functional on both views – StocksPage and StockDetails views.

Implementing the State Persistence

So far, you can add and remove the stocks at run time while you are running the application. As soon as you come out of the application and rerun it, the added stocks information is not saved, and you will go back to the default application state with MSFT stock available as a default stock.

As a part of state persistence, we will persist the stock details to CSV file in the application local storage. For this we will use *WinJS.Application.local* object to store and retrieve the file. We will develop two additional functions, *SaveStocks* and *LoadStocks* function, in the existing JavaScript *LocalStorageHelper* class to implement such functionality.

The SaveStocks Function

The *SaveStocks* function will convert the *Stock* list into CSV string and then uses the *WinJS.Application.local.WriteText* function to write file to the application local storage saved with the name *StocksFile.csv* file.

The following is a complete code of this function, which you need to add just after the *GetRandomStockData* function exists in the *LocalStorageHelper.js* file, which is available under the *Common* folder.

141

```
stockFile: "StocksFile.csv",
csvString: "",
SaveStocks: function () {
    var app = WinJS.Application;
    FinanceHub.Data.Stocks.forEach(showIteration);
    function showIteration(value, index, array) {
        var temp = [];
        temp.push(value.Symbol);
        temp.push(value.OpenPrice);
        temp.push(value.CurrentPrice);
        temp.push(value.Change);
        temp.push(value.DaysRange);
        temp.push(value.Range52Week);
        FinanceHub.LocalStorageHelper.csvString =
            FinanceHub.LocalStorageHelper.csvString.concat(temp.join(),
"\r\n");
    }

    app.local.writeText(FinanceHub.LocalStorageHelper.stockFile,
        FinanceHub.LocalStorageHelper.csvString);
},
```

The LoadStocks Function

The *LoadStocks* function will read the *StocksFile.csv* created by *SaveStocks* function.

The following is a complete code of this function, which you need to add just after the *SaveStocks* function exists in the *LocalStorageHelper.js* file, which is available under the *Common* folder.

```
LoadStocks: function () {
    var app = WinJS.Application;

    return app.local.exists(FinanceHub.LocalStorageHelper.stockFile).
then(function (exists)
    {
        if (exists)
            return app.local.readText(FinanceHub.LocalStorageHelper.
stockFile).then(function (data)
            {
                return FinanceHub.LocalStorageHelper.ParseCSV(data);
            });
        else return null;
    });
},
```

Check State Persistence

You will save the added/removed stocks when application is suspended or shut down by placing the following code within the *app.oncheckpoint* event handler that exists in the *default.js* file, which is available under the *js* folder:

```
app.oncheckpoint = function (args) {
    // TODO: This application is about to be suspended. Save any state
    // that needs to persist across suspensions here. If you need to
    // complete an asynchronous operation before your application is
    // suspended, call args.setPromise().
    app.sessionState.history = nav.history;

    FinanceHub.LocalStorageHelper.SaveStocks();
};
```

▪ **Note** The *Suspend and Shutdown* option from the Debug Control menu appears only while you are running the project. For some reason, if you do not find this option while you are debugging the project, go to *Tools/Customize* option and select the *Debug Location* Toolbar item.

To restore the stocks back, we need to modify the function for *WinJS.Binding. processAll* in the *default.js*, as following highlighted code:

```
WinJS.Binding.processAll(document.body, pageVM).then(function () {

    //Load previous state
    FinanceHub.LocalStorageHelper.LoadStocks().then(function (csvData) {
        if (csvData != null && csvData.length > 0) {
            csvData.forEach(showIteration);
        }
        else {
            FinanceHub.Data.Stocks.push(FinanceHub.Command.
GetNewStock("MSFT"));
        }

        function showIteration(value, index, array) {
            if (value != "") {
                FinanceHub.Data.Stocks.push(new FinanceHub.Model.Stock
                    (value[0], value[1], value[2], value[3], value[4],
value[5]));
            }
        }
    }).then(function () {
```

```
        // Activates knockout.js
        ko.applyBindings(new FinanceHub.ViewModel.
AddRemoveStockViewModel());
    });
});
```

Note   At this point, for the first time when you compile and run the project, you may get an error while application tries to first load previous state. This is potentially a defect with the current WinRT RC release. The solution I have found is first to comment out the code that you just wrote within the *WinJS.Binding.processAll* function to restore the stocks back in the default.js file; then line and run the project. At this time you should not get any error. Now, select the *Suspend and Shutdown* option from the Debug Control menu (which appears only while you are running the project), which will suspend and then shut down the application. Revisit the commented code and uncomment, and from this time onward, you should not be getting any error.

Congratulations! You have finished the development of Windows8 FinanceHub application using the JavaScript and HTML5 and following the MVVM design pattern! Run the project (follow the above note if you are getting an error), and you should see all implemented functionalities working, including the added/removed stocks saved into the local storage. Then upon application startup, the stored stocks will be retrieved and will get assigned random values.

Summary

This is the final chapter of the book. In this chapter you created a navigation template-based Windows 8 JavaScript application project and set up the structure to support MVVM-based implementation. Later we developed the View, Model, and ViewModel of the FinanceHub application with all features that were also implemented using XAML and C# in the earlier chapters of this book.

This chapter demonstrates that Windows 8 application platform is versatile, supporting different development platforms, including JavaScript and HTML5, and can follow the best and recommended design patterns such as MVVM.

Do not forget to download the source code. Visit the Chapter 6 folder to look at the source code that we developed in this chapter. This chapter has a special source code structure. You will find the code for only View, ViewModel, and Model implementation and then for the complete project in related folders.

You have started an exciting journey of Windows 8 application development, and I hope this book successfully guides you along it. I wish you good luck.

Index

W, X, Y, Z

204

www.ingramcontent.com/pod-product-compliance
Ingram Content Group UK Ltd.
Pitfield, Milton Keynes, MK11 3LW, UK
UKHW020212231225
466357UK00011B/110